The Fairies and The Christmas Child

[ILLUSTRATED]

The Fairies and The Christmas Child

[ILLUSTRATED]

Lilian Gask

Illustrator: Willy Pogány

ILLUSTRATED &
PUBLISHED BY
E-KİTAP PROJESİ & CHEAPEST BOOKS

www.cheapestboooks.com

 www.facebook.com/EKitapProjesi

Istanbul

ISBN: 978-605-7876-93-5

The Fairies
and The Christ
·mas Child·

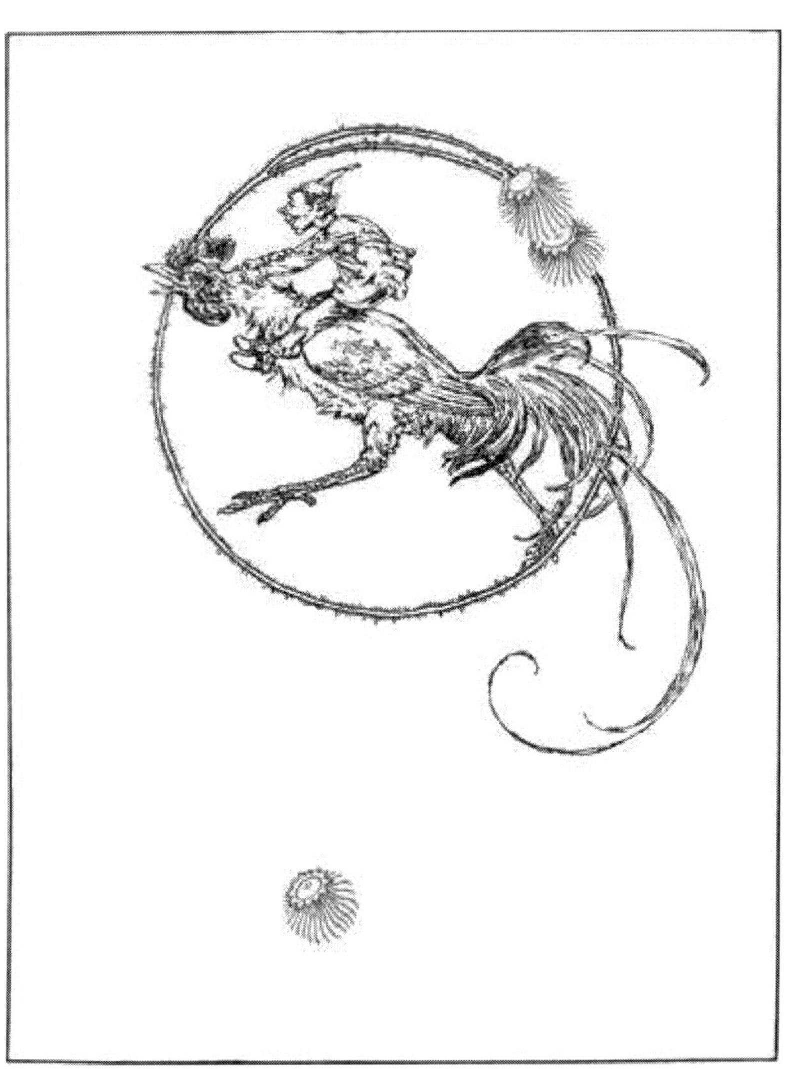

Fr. "We rocked the cradle"

The
Fairies and
the Christmas Child
By Lilian Gask
The Illustrations are by
Willy Pogány
T.Y. Crowell & Co
New York

To
"The Doctor"
and
Mrs. Macnaughton-Jones
my "Good Fairies"
and best of
Friends

The worst of being a Christmas Child is that you don't get birthday presents, but only Christmas ones. Old Naylor, who was Father's coachman, and had a great gruff voice that came from his boots and was rather frightening, used to ask how I expected to grow up without proper birthdays, and I thought I might have to stay little always. When I told Father this he laughed, but a moment later he grew quite grave.

"Listen, Chris," he said. And then he took me on his knee—I was a small chap then—and told me things that made me forget old Naylor, and wish and wish that Mother could have stayed with us. The angels had wanted her, Father explained; well, we wanted her too, and there were plenty of angels in heaven, anyway. When I said this Father gave me a great squeeze and put me down, and I tried to be glad that I was a Christmas child. But I wasn't really until a long time afterwards, when I had found the Fairy Ring, and met the Queen of the Fairies.

This was how it happened. Father and I lived at one end of a big town, in a funny old house with an orchard behind it, where the sparrows ate the cherries and the apple trees didn't flower. Once upon a time, said Father, there had been country all round it, but the streets and the roads had grown and grown until they drove the country away, and now there were trams outside the door, and not a field to be seen. I often thought that our garden must be sorry to be so crowded up, and that this was why it wouldn't grow anything but weedy nasturtiums and evening primroses.

Father is a doctor, and most awfully clever. If you cut off the top of your finger, he'd pop it on again in no time, and he used to cure all sorts of illnesses with different coloured medicines he made himself behind a screen.

But though he had lots and lots of patients—sometimes the surgery was full of them, 'specially on cold nights when there was a fire—they didn't seem to have much money to give him, and sometimes they ran away with their furniture in the night so's not to pay their bills. This worried Father dreadfully, and even Santa Claus was scared away by the things he said. On Christmas Eve the old fellow quite forgot to fill my stocking. It was all limp and empty when I woke in the morning, and if I hadn't remembered that when I grew up I was going to be a Commander-in-Chief, I should never have swallowed that lump in my throat.

Father couldn't even take me to hear "Hark The Herald Angels" at the big church down the road that day, for someone sent for him in a hurry, and when he didn't come in for dinner, I wished it wasn't Christmas at all. Nancy Blake, who kept house for us and was most stingy over raisins, banged the kitchen door when I said I would make her some toffee, and I couldn't find anything else to do. I looked at all my books and pretended I was a soldier in a lonely fort; then I thought I would make up medicine myself, so's to save Father trouble when he came home. But I burnt my fingers with some nasty stuff in a green bottle, and it hurt a good deal. So I determined to go to meet him, and tell him what I'd done.

"Nancy Blake."

The trams were running as usual, and as I had a penny left out of my pocket money—I hadn't spent it before as it had got stuck in some bulls' eyes—I took the car to the corner; then I jumped out and walked. There wasn't a sign of Father all down the road, and I remembered at last that he had said he must look in at the Hospital, which was in quite a different direction. I should have gone home then, if it hadn't been so dull with no one but Nancy Blake.

"He won't be back until tea time anyhow," I thought, and I made up my mind to be a boy scout, and go and explore.

It was a splendid day, and the roofs of the shops and houses glittered from millions of tiny points, just as you see on Christmas cards. I walked on and on, feeling gladder every moment, for my fingers had left off hurting me and I knew that I couldn't be far from the woods, which were just outside the town. I had been there once with Father, and it was lovely; so I hurried on as quickly as I could.

When I got there they made me think of Fairyland. The trees were sparkling with the same frost-diamonds I had noticed on the roofs, and through the criss-cross branches above my head the sky was as blue as blue. A jolly little robin was twittering in a bush, enjoying himself no end; his bright red breast reminded me of the holly I had stuck over Father's mantelpiece, and I began to feel sad again. For it did seem hard lines that though Christmas was my birthday, no one, not even Father, had thought of it.

"I wish that I hadn't been born on Christmas Day!" I said aloud, when I had reached the very heart of the wood, and I sat down to rest on the stump of a tree close to a little circle of bright green. It was here I had come that day with Father, and he had told me that though it was called a "Fairy Ring," it was really made by the spread of a very small fungus, or mushroom. I liked the idea of the fairy ring much better, and as I touched it with my foot I wished again that I wasn't a Christmas child. And then I heard a sigh.

It wasn't the robin, for he was still twittering on his bush, and it wasn't the wind, for the air was quite sheltered behind the bank, which was sweet with wild thyme in summer. The next moment I heard another sigh, and this seemed to come from a frond of bracken just outside the fairy ring. It was brown and withered, but the frost had silvered it all over, and as I looked at it I saw the loveliest little creature you can imagine clinging to the stem. She was only about three inches high, but her tiny form was full of grace, and her eyes so bright and beautiful that they shone like stars. Her hair was the palest silver-gold, and she had a crown of diamonds and an amethyst wand that sparkled when she moved it. The scarf wreathed round her shoulders flashed all the colours of mother-of-pearl, and throwing it from her she hummed to herself a little song about violets and eglantine, and sweet musk roses. Her notes were as clear as the lark's, and as if she had called them, more Fairies showed amidst the bracken.

They were lovely too, though not so lovely as she. One was dressed in pink, like a pink pea; another had a long grey coat, spangled with drops of dew, while the third had wings like a big grey moth, and the smallest Elf was all in brown.

"It is Titania who sings," chirped the robin in my left ear; "Titania, the Queen of the Fairies, though some call her the fair Queen Mab!" And he hopped to the foot of the frond of bracken and made a funny little duck with his head.

"Good bird!" cried Titania, breaking off her song. "You, too, sing through the winter gloom, and are here to welcome the sweet o' the year." Then she pointed her gleaming wand at me, and shook her head.

"O Christmas child," she said reproachfully, "it is well that it was I who heard you, and not my brave lord Oberon, who has less patience with mortal folly. So you wish you had not been born on Christmas Day? Why, 'tis the day most blessed in all the year—the day when the King of Kings sent peace and goodwill to Man in the form of the Christ Child. It is His birthday as well as yours, and in memory of Him the Fairies show themselves to Christmas children, if they are pure in heart and word and deed. Your Mother knew this, and she was glad. She called you 'Chris' to remind you always which day you came."

And then I was sure that I hadn't been dreaming after all, though Nancy said, "Stuff and Nonsense," when I fancied that I had seen those wee brown men busy about the house on winter mornings, or flitting in shadowy corners at night, before she lit the gas. I had never spoken to them, for I thought if I did they might run away; but I was pleased to know they had been real.

"You would have seen us before," said Titania, "but you live in a big town, and your eyes were dimmed with smoke and fog. My dainty Elves love dales and streams, and the depths of forests; in spring they throng the meadows, decking the cowslips' coats of gold at early dawn with splotches of ruby, my choicest favours, and hanging pearls in their dainty ears. In summer they sleep in the roseleaves, and ride behind the wings of butterflies, while in winter they hush the babble of the brooks, and powder the branches of the trees with frost to hide their nakedness. Away with you, Peas-blossom, Cobweb, Moth, and Mustard-seed! Go, freeze the fingers of Father Time into glassy icicles, and forget not to seek for crimson berries on which our friends the birds may feed at morn!"

I fancied that I had seen those wee brown men

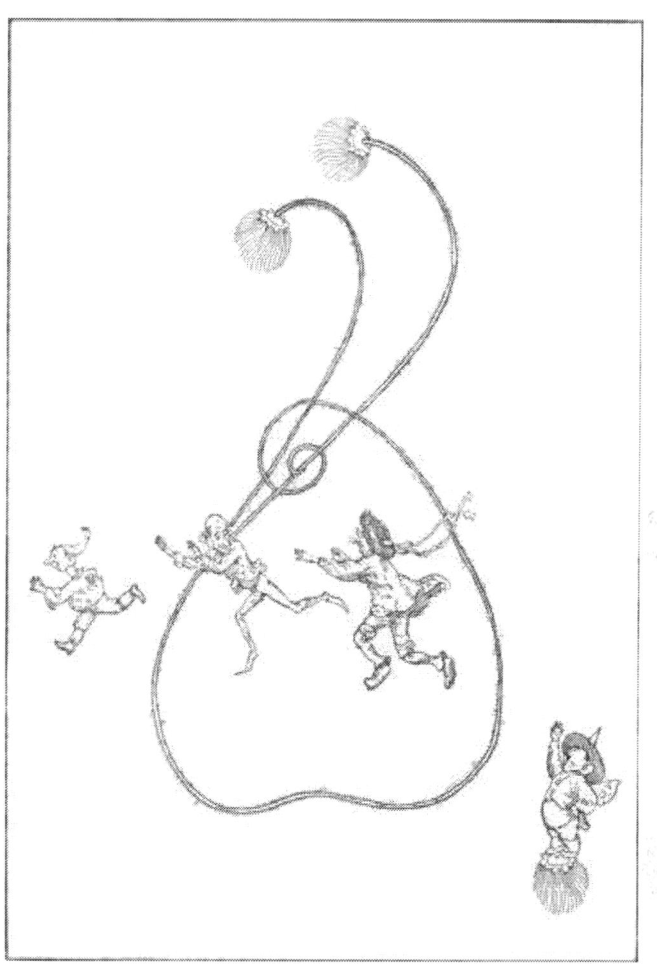

She clapped her hands, and the Fairies fled. I wondered why she did not fall, since she no longer clung to the frond of bracken; but her tiny feet were firmly planted in the fork of a leaf, and behind her glinted a pair of wings which had been invisible before. As I watched her I thought of a question I had often wanted to ask.

"Where do Fairies come from?" I said, hoping she would not be offended.

"Ah," she replied, "that is more than I may tell you. But we were here, in these very islands, long before the people of the woods, and the white-haired Druids who worshipped the God of the Oak. There were spirits then, as now, in streams and rivers, and sweet-voiced Sirens in the deep blue sea. Some Fairies rode on magic horses, and some were even smaller than I, and lived in the ears of the yellow corn. Dagda then was the King of the Fairies, a mighty spirit whose cauldron was supposed to be the vast grey dome of the sky. Those were the days of Witches, Dwarfs, and Giants, and little people who lived in the hills, and many other Fairies known by different names.

We are found in various guises all over the world, but our home is said first to have been in Persia. There dwelt the ancient Jinn who haunted the mountain recesses and the forest wilds ages before the first man trod the earth. Here, too, were Deevs, malicious creatures of terrible strength who warred with our sisters, the Peries. These exquisite creatures abode at Kâf, in the deep green mountains of Chrysolite, the realm of Pleasure and Delight, wherein was the beauteous Amber City. Some day you may go to Persia, and then, if you meet a Peri, she will tell you how a mortal man once came to her sisters' rescue, and conquered the wicked Deevs."

The thought of meeting a Peri took my breath away, for I had read about them on winter evenings.

"Do you mean that wherever I go I shall see the Fairies, just as I see you now?" I cried.

"Wherever you go!" she said, nodding her head, "and soon I believe you will cross the sea and travel through other lands. But you must not think," she went on earnestly, "that the Fairies in your own country are less worth knowing, for you might spend your life in making friends with them, and yet have much to learn."

I can't remember half of all that Titania told me after this, but she spoke of fair White Elves who live among the trees, and are ruled by a King who rides abroad in a beautiful little coach with trappings of gold and silver; of mischievous Black Elves who live underground, and haunt people with nasty tempers; of Nymphs and Gnomes and sad-faced Trolls, and of Brownies and Portunes and Pixies. I should have liked to hear more about the Brownies and Portunes, but it was fun to learn how the Brownies play tricks on lazy people who lie in bed and won't get up, pulling the clothes right off them, and throwing these on the floor, and of how they help the farmers' wives to bake and brew if they are clean and neat. Titania said that Fairies dislike people who are untidy, and I hoped that she hadn't seen my playbox or my chest of drawers. I made up my mind that directly I got home I would put them straight, and so that she might not notice how red I had grown, I asked her to tell me what Portunes were.

The "Portunes" were queer creatures.

"Queer little wrinkled creatures with faces like old men," she said. "They wear long green coats covered with darns and patches, and are only found now in the depths of the country. They like to live on prosperous farms, and though some of them are barely an inch high, they can lift heavier weights than the strongest labourer. Like the Brownies, they can be mischievous as well as helpful. A farmer once offended a Portune by speaking disrespectfully of his kindred, and the next time that the good man rode home from market in the dusk, the little fellow sprang on to the horse's reins, and guided him into the bog. Both horse and man had to flounder out as best they could, and the farmer was careful henceforth to mind his tongue."

"And what are Pixies like?" I asked. She had said that I reminded her of one of these, so of course I was curious about them.

"They are much taller than we are, and very fair," answered Titania, "with blue-grey eyes like yours. If you want to meet them, you must go to Devonshire, for it is there that they make their home. They love the ferns and the heather, and the rich red earth, and live in a Pixy-house in a rock. They, also, are ruled by a King, who commands them as I do my Elves and Fays, despatching them hither and thither to do his will. Sometimes he sends them down to the mines, to show the men who work there where the richest lode is to be found; and if the miners grumble, or are discontented, the Pixies lead them astray by lighting false fires. On other occasions they are told off to help the villagers with their housework, and their attentions are warmly welcomed by the Devon folk. One good dame was so pleased with the help a ragged little Pixie who had torn her frock on a sweet-briar bush gave her with her spinning, that she made her a new set of clothes of bright green cloth, and laid these by the spinning wheel. The Pixy put them on at once, and singing

"Pixy fine, Pixy gay,
Pixy now will run away!"

sped out of the house in broad daylight, and, alas! she never came back again."

"Ho! ho! ho!" laughed a merry voice, and a shock-headed little fellow swung himself down from a bough just behind me, and turned a somersault on the ground.

"Welcome, gay Puck!" Titania cried. "Whence do you come, and what do you do this night?"

"I come from the court of King Oberon, sweet Titania," answered the Elf, "and to-night I plait the manes and tails of Farmer Best's grey horses. At early dawn I shall skim the cream off the milk in his good wife's dairy, since yester-e'en she grudged a drink of it to an orphan child. 'Robin Goodfellow has been here!' she will cry when she sees what I have been after, and her greedy old eyes will fill with tears. That is one of my pet names, Wide-eyes," he added, hopping on to my shoulder and pinching my ear. "I am also Pouke, Hobgoblin, and Robin Hood. But where are the Urchins, my merry play-fellows? It is high time that they were here, for the lady moon has hung her lamp i' the sky."

"The Fairy Ring was thronged with dancing Elves"

The clouds were all tinted a deep rose pink, and behind the trees, just where the moon had risen, was a haze of purple. I knew by this that it must be nearly tea-time, and I was just going to say that I must go, when Titania left the frond of bracken, and alighted in the centre of the Fairy Ring. Waving her wand, she summoned her "gladsome sprites," and next moment the Fairy Ring was thronged with dancing Elves who wore red caps and silver shoes, with bright green mantles buttoned with bobs of silk. Puck flew to join them, but Peas-blossom, Cobweb, Moth, and Mustard-seed, who sprang from nowhere, danced in an inner circle round the Fairy Queen. They sang as they danced, and this is their song. I found it afterwards in a book of Father's, which he said had in it more wonderful things than all books in the world but one:

"By the moon we sport and play,
With the night begins our day.
As we frisk the dew doth fall,
Trip it, little urchins all.
Lightly as the little bee,
Two by two and three by three,
And about goe wee, goe wee."

"And about goe wee, goe wee!" echoed down the glade, and then the Elves suddenly disappeared, with Puck and Titania and her attendants.

The wood was growing darker every minute, but the sparkles of frost were glittering still, and lit my way. At the end of the scrub I saw Father coming to meet me, swinging down the road with such long steps that he looked like a kindly big giant. He had guessed where I had gone, and he was so pleased to find me that he forgot to say I mustn't explore any more without him, as I was afraid he would. He took my hand, and we both ran; it was lovely at home by the fire.

I meant to have told him about Queen Titania while we were having tea, but Nancy had made such scrumptious cakes that there wasn't time at first, and before I had finished he began to open the letters that had come just after he left that morning. They seemed to be all bills, and Father sighed as he looked them over, his forehead puckered into rucks and lines. Presently he came to a big blue envelope, and he turned this round and round as if he thought there might be something horrid inside. The paper crackled like anything as he drew it out, and when it was unfolded he sat looking at it for a long time, though there didn't seem to be much writing. At last he gave an odd kind of gasp, and took my face between his hands. He pressed it so hard that he made me say "O!" though I didn't want to do this, and I wondered what had happened.

"Your great-aunt Helen is dead, Chris," he said at last, as he let me go. "I haven't seen her for years and years.... She was not over kind to me when I was a lad, though I believe she meant well.... And now she's left us all her money. We shan't be poor any more."

This was the beginning of ever so many surprises. First, Father and I had warm new overcoats, with woolly stuff inside them that felt like blankets, only much more soft and fluffy, and Nancy had the blue silk dress she always vowed that she should buy when her ship came home. There was a fire every night in Father's study, and I had one in my bedroom. More patients came up for soup than they did for medicine, and they said "God bless you, Sir!" to Father so often that he wanted to run away. The children in the hospital had the biggest tree that the ward would hold, and all the old men and women in the workhouse had a big tea, and shawls and mufflers.

A few weeks later a strange young man with a very shiny collar and a new brown bag came to stay with us. Father said he was a "locum," but Nancy said it ought to be "locust," for his appetite was enormous, and she couldn't make enough buttered toast to please him. He had come to take care of Father's patients until someone bought all the medicines and things in the surgery, and I was awfully glad to hear we were going away.

"We'll go straight to the sunshine, Chris," said Father, "where there are trees and flowers instead of long rows of houses, and the air isn't full of smoke."

And that night I dreamt all about fairies, and of what I was going to see and hear in foreign lands.

The "Locust."

The cliffs were hidden in the mist when we left Dover, and the sky was dull and grey. But very soon it began to clear; a silvery light shone behind the clouds, and then the sun came out, and the rolling waves turned emerald green. They tossed our steamer up and down as if it were a cork, and Father soon went below, but I begged so hard to be allowed to stay on deck that he said I might if I would promise, "honour bright," not to get into mischief.

When he had gone I put my cap into my pocket, so that it might not blow off, and leaned over the rails to watch the swell of the sea. I wasn't thinking of Fairies then, nor of being a Christmas child, but of how it must feel to be shipwrecked. So when the spray blew in my face and made me blink, I was surprised to see a merry red face grinning up at me from the foam. It had curls of seaweed upon its forehead, and a mouth like a big round "O".

"I'm Father Neptune," it roared, so loudly that I could hear it quite distinctly above the noise of the wind. "Why not take a header, and come and ride one of my fine sea horses? 'Father wouldn't like it?' Ho! ho! ho! What a molly-coddle of a boy!"

A big wave tossed him on one side, and on its crest was a beautiful girl with a shining tail, and hair like a stream of gold. Of course I knew she was a mermaid, and would want me to go to her coral caves.

"Won't you come with me and play with my sheeny pearls?" she cried. "They gleam like the dawn on a summer morning, and you shall choose the loveliest for your very own."

She held out her arms and I nearly sprang into them, for I thought that a pearl would be splendid for Father's pin. But just behind her I saw two ugly mermen, with horrid green teeth and bright red eyes, and ropes of seaweed in their long thin hands. Then I remembered that mermaids were dangerous, and I ran straight over to the other side of the steamer and put my fingers into my ears, so that I might not hear her call. She spoke so sweetly that it was difficult to resist, but I did not trust her.

The water was calmer on this side, and I wondered why until I saw some funny brown men, rather like Brownies, but ever so much bigger and stronger, stretched out at full length on the tops of the waves. They were blowing on conchs as hard as they could, and wherever they blew, the waves grew quieter. I guessed at once that they were Tritons—seafolk who live with Neptune in his crystal palace under the sea. I was still watching them when Father came up behind me, and told me that we were really in.

We stayed the night at a big hotel where almost everyone spoke in a language which I did not understand, and I had a grown-up dinner with Father, with heaps of different dishes, most of them tasting much alike. Next day we went on for hours in the train, and the air grew warmer and warmer, and the grass more green, until at last we were in the south of France. There were palms and orange groves and heaps of flowers, and it would have been just splendid if Father had been all right. He hadn't had time to be ill at home you see, and now there were no sick people to worry him, he was so tired that he couldn't do anything. But he told me not to worry, for once he was really rested, he would soon get well.

And so he did, though it took a long time to rest him, and we couldn't explore a bit. In the mornings we strolled through the gardens, or down to the sea, and most afternoons we did nothing at all. Very often, as I sat beside him on the verandah, with the sun shining full on the green awning, and the roses nodding to us over the balcony, he would fall asleep; and then a Flower-Fairy would peep through the ferns, and tell me the loveliest stories. The Rose-Fairy came, and the Queen of the Lilies, with a lovely gold crown upon her head; but my favourite Fairy lived in a bed of violets. Her frock was purple, and I knew when she was coming because the air all round grew sweet. Her stories were the best of all. She had heard them from the wind, she said, as he played with her leaves at dawn. My favourite was one that she said he had brought from Provence.

The Princess with the Sea-Green Hair.

"A worthy couple at Marseilles," she began, "had longed for a child for years in vain, and great was their joy when they knew at last that their wish was about to be granted. The boy was born during a fearful storm, and the first sound he heard was the crash of the sea as it broke on the shore. He was christened Paul, and grew up into a handsome lad with a quantity of thick fair hair which curled like the tips of the waves, and piercing blue eyes which were always twinkling with fun and mischief.

There was not any question as to what calling he should follow, for the sea claimed him as a son of her own, and he was never content on dry land. When his ship came home and the crew was dismissed, he could not rest, and every evening at sunset he would row himself out in a little boat as far as he could go. One summer night, when a thousand ripples danced on the waves, he leaned over the side of his boat, gazing down—down—down. He did not know why, but he felt quite sure that someone was calling him, and with all his heart he longed to obey the summons. Presently he felt himself lifted gently, and drawn through the gleaming water by hands which he could not see. It was black as night before they released him, for neither sun nor moon pierce the depths of the ocean. He would have been in total darkness but for the strange-shaped fish who carried lanterns on their heads, and guided him to the gates of a palace, formed of millions of barnacles. These were piled one on the top of the other until they reached an enormous height, and were decorated with what looked like a row of human eyes.

The gates flew open as Paul approached them, and through a passage of mother-of-pearl he reached a chamber that flashed with opal lights. Here a Fairy Princess awaited him—a Princess so exquisitely beautiful in spite of her sea-green hair, that though his heart did not go out to her, he was not repelled by the love she showed him.

She kept him with her for many hours, and at dawn of day she bade him return to his home, giving him two golden fish which he was to show to all who asked him where he had spent the night, telling them he had been a'fishing. The invisible hands which had brought him thither bore him back to his boat, and he landed just at sunrise. His golden fish were a source of awe and wonder to his neighbours, who had never seen their like before; but the priest shook his head, and warned him to have no dealings with the powers of darkness.

Here a Fairy Princess awaited him—

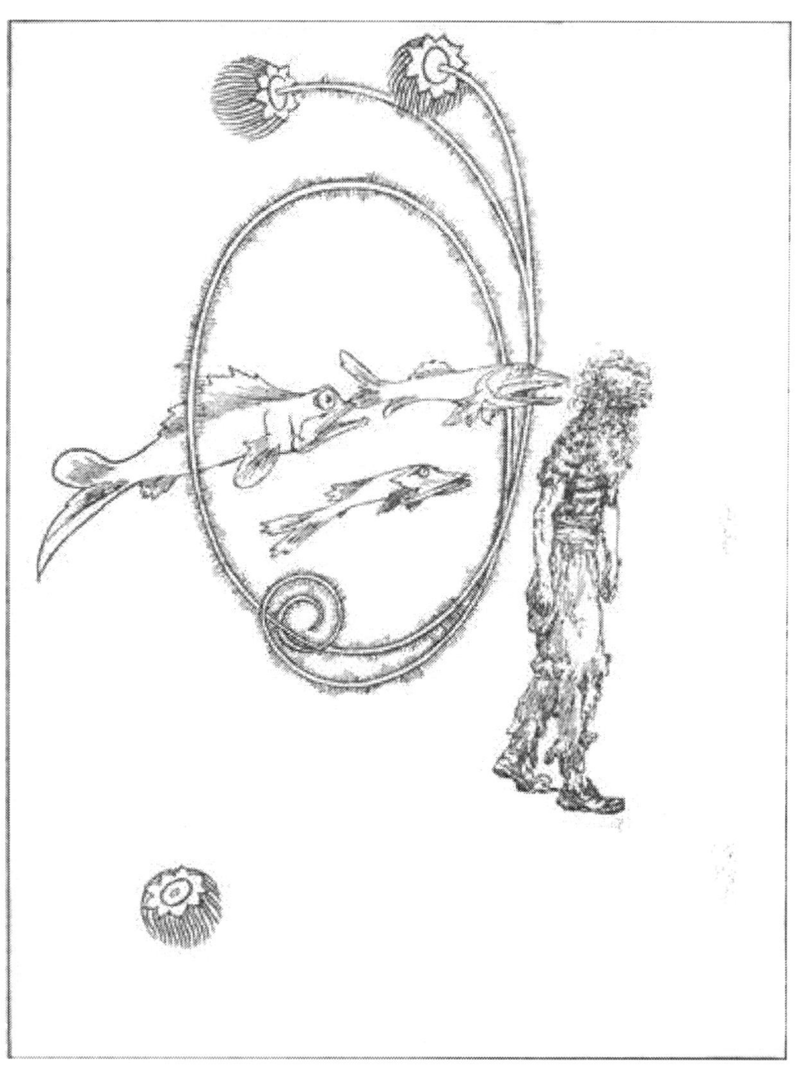

But Paul could not resist rowing out to the edge of the sunset. Evening after evening he plied his oars, and always at twilight he was drawn down—down, to the palace of the strange Princess with the sea-green hair. When he went on a voyage all was well with him, for his vessel bore him to other seas, where no one called him when the sky grew red; but he was no sooner at home with his parents than something within him made him row out to the west.

At last it seemed as if he had forgotten the Princess, for he fell in love with sweet Lucile, who was as good and gentle as she was fair, and willingly gave him her troth. Their wedding was fixed for Easter Day, and the night before, Paul wandered down to the sea-shore, thinking of the bliss in store for him on the morrow. His love-lit eyes fell dreamily on his boat, which had lain for months in the shallow cove where he had moored her, and without thinking what he was doing, he stepped inside and took the oars in his hands. Alas! No sooner did he feel the boat moving under him, than he was seized by the old wild longing to sail towards the west.

All happened as before, until he reached the Princess's palace; but now, instead of smiling sweetly, she received him with threatening looks which showed an array of cruel teeth behind her rose-red lips.

'So! you have been unfaithful to me!' she cried. 'I will not slay you, since I have greater punishments in store than death.... You shall stay in the depths of the sea until your yellow hair is bleached and white, and your face a mask of hideous wrinkles. Then, and then only, shall you return to land, and those who have loved you best shall spurn you from them as something loathsome. Scorn for scorn, and pain for pain. Thus will I take my revenge.'

So for seven long years Paul was a prisoner in the darkness of the deep, his bed the black and slimy ooze, and his companions fearsome monsters who would fain have devoured him. At last, when his hair was white as snow, and his face so wrinkled and ugly that the children of the mer-folk shuddered as they passed, he was seized by a sprawling octopus, and dragged up through the water. The loathsome creature held him fast until they reached a spot not far from the little brown cottage where Lucile had lived with her old father, and here it loosened its coils; and a great wave cast Paul on shore. The cottage was empty and deserted, and the winding path he had trodden so often was covered with moss. Close by, however, was another cottage, far more spacious, and through the open door of this Paul saw his old sweetheart sitting beside a cradle. She sang as she rocked it gently with her foot, and her shining needles flew in and out of a fisherman's coarse blue sock.

As the shadow fell across the threshold she looked up brightly, expecting to see her husband. Meeting Paul's gaze instead, her own grew strained with horror, and snatching her baby from the cradle she fled to the inner room. Without a word Paul hastened away. He knew his doom, and hastened to throw himself back to the sea.

In his headlong flight he stumbled against an old, old woman, gathering drift-wood on the wreck-strewn coast. She would have fallen if he had not caught her in his arms, and as he held her she saw his eyes. They alone were unchanged, and his mother knew them.

'My boy—my dear boy!' she cried with a sob of joy. And she drew his seared face down to her bosom, murmuring over it the same fond words she had used when he was a child. She kissed him, and the spell was broken; once more he was good to look upon.... The Princess had not known, you see, that a mother's love is immortal."

Father was still asleep when the story came to an end, so I implored the Fairy to tell me another.

"This comes from Provence, too," she said in answer to my pleading, "and will show you that sea-folk can sometimes be merciful."

The Sailor and the Porpoise.

"Among the crew of the good ship *L'Oiseau*, was a sailor named Antoine, who kept all on board alive with his merry wit. One day, while sailing the waters of the Mediterranean, the sea only faintly ruffled by the breeze that helped them on their way, they espied what at first appeared to be a huge sea-serpent making its way towards them. For a few moments the mariners watched it in much alarm; then, to their immense relief, they found that their 'sea-serpent' was a string of harmless porpoises, swimming in a row, with their shining black backs just appearing above the surface of the water. As they neared the ship they broke their ranks, and evidently regarding the sailors as their friends, gambolled upon the waves like boisterous children. No man dreamt of interfering with them until Antoine thoughtlessly picked up a rusty spear and threw it at one of those farthest away. He did not do this from any desire to kill, but only to show how excellent was his aim, and when he saw his shaft strike home, tinging the sea with red as his victim sank with a convulsive shudder, he was seized with self-reproach and a nameless dread.

And behold! a great storm shook the sea, as if the gods themselves were angry. Thunder and lightning rolled and flashed, and raindrops heavy as leaden balls fell in swift torrents. So fearful was the tempest that it threatened to overwhelm the ship, and the Captain was in despair.

In this dire extremity a knight on a magnificent black charger came riding over the waves.

'Surrender him who threw the spear!' he cried, and the sea stayed its turmoil to listen. 'Do this, and I will save the ship. Else shall it perish, with all on board, and sea creatures shall gnaw your bones.'

The sailors were exceedingly afraid, but they would not betray their comrade. Seeing this, Antoine stepped forth of his own accord, for he would not let his shipmates suffer for his fault. Leaping from the deck, he landed upon the haunches of the charger, behind the knight, and that moment the sea became smooth as glass, and the strange steed disappeared with his two riders.

The ship made good way, and his shipmates never expected to see poor Antoine again, but to the amazement and joy of all, he rejoined the vessel a few days later as though it had stood by for him. The excitement of the men was great as they gathered round him to hear of his adventures.

And truly he had a marvellous story to relate. He had ridden, he told them, to a distant island, where in a castle of shimmering gold, on a bed of the softest eiderdown, he found a knight stretched in agony. It was he whom he had wounded, while in the form of a porpoise, and the spear he had thrown so thoughtlessly was still sticking in his side. He drew this out, with tears of shame, and then, with his guilty right hand, he cleansed and bathed the wound. When this was done, the knight fell into a deep sleep, and woke at dawn well as ever. Taking Antoine's hand, he led him through many corridors lit with gems to a resplendent banquet hall, where the walls were encrusted with star-shaped sapphires, and the floor was of beaten gold. Many other knights were assembled here, and maidens so fair that Antoine sighed to think of them. When he had feasted on curious dishes of rich fruits, the same knight who had brought him thither took him back to the sea-shore, where the same black horse awaited their coming. Mounting as before, the charger sped like the wind over the sea until the ship hove in sight. When they came to within one hundred yards of the vessel, the black steed and his rider disappeared as mysteriously as they had come, and Antoine was left struggling in the water. However, he was an excellent swimmer, and soon reached the ship's side, up which he easily clambered by the aid of a rope which fortunately happened to be trailing in the water.

This was the tale that Antoine told his shipmates, and in memory of the clemency of the porpoise-knight, the sailors vowed that never again would they injure a porpoise. Not only were they as good as their word, but the vow is kept to this day by their children's children."

It was spring time when we left for Brittany. Father had been there once with Mother, and thought he would like to go again. So I said goodbye to my Flower-Fairy, and promised that if I could I would come back one day to see her.

The sunny air of the south had done Father good, and now he was almost well. While we were in the train he read from the guide book, and told me about curious "dolmens," or mounds of stone, which are supposed to have been built to mark the ancients' burying places. There were hundreds of these in Brittany, he said, and I was glad, for I knew they were haunted by "Gorics" and "Courils"—strange Fairies of olden times.

That very first evening, while Father was writing letters, I slipped away by myself instead of going to bed, for I wanted to see a Poupican. A Poupican, you must know, is the dwarf-child of a Korrigan—a Fairy who looks lovely by night and horrible by day, and cares for nothing so that she gets what she wants. Korrigans are said to have been princesses in days gone by, but they were so cruel and selfish that someone laid them under a spell, which lasts for thousands of years unless a mortal breaks it. On account of the wicked things they said their mouths are always dry, and they are consumed by thirst; so they chose their homes by streams and fountains, of which there are many in Brittany.

Father had been telling me that there was a famous fountain in a wood not far from our hotel, and I thought I might find them here. The fountain was hidden behind a grove of fir-trees, but the moon shone down on its rough grey stones, and turned the square pond of water in front of it into a silver mirror.

At first there seemed to be no one there, but when my eyes had grown used to the gloom I saw a number of Elves about two feet in height, with misty white veils wound round their bodies. A cloth was spread beside the fountain. It was covered with the loveliest things to eat—honey and fruit, and queer-shaped cakes sprinkled with sugar comfits—while in the centre stood a crystal goblet, from which the moon drew flashes of soft fairy light. As I crouched in the ferns, a wee green Wood-Elf stole up behind me; her tiny face was good and kind, and although she was so small that I could almost have held her in my hand, I felt she was there to protect me.

Then I turned my eyes to the crystal goblet and I grew thirsty all at once; and I wondered what the Korrigans would do if I took a sip of the amber wine which filled it to the brim.

"One drop would make you wise for ever," whispered the Wood-Elf, just as if I had spoken, "but you would be silent for ever, also. No mortal can drink that wine and live. The Korrigans pass it round to each other in a golden cup at the end of their feast, which takes place but once in the year. It gives them power to work many charms, and to take the form of animals at will."

The Hunter who shot the white Doe.

"Once, in these very woods, a hunter shot a fair white doe, when to his amazement, she spoke to him in a human voice. He was so touched by her reproaches that he tore his fine linen shirt into strips to bind up her wound, and then hurried off to the spring for water to quench her thirst. It was dusk by the time he could get back to her, for the first spring he reached was dry, and instead of the milk-white doe, he found a beauteous maiden, who threw herself on his bosom and entreated him not to leave her.

For a year and a day he was under her spells, but he escaped in the end by making the sign of the cross with his two forefingers. This sign puts a Korrigan to instant flight, for things which are holy fill them with terror.... Ah! they have been at their mischief again. Poor Annette will weep for this."

The Wood-Elf stopped speaking, for running lightly over the grass, holding each other's long white veils so as to form a swinging cradle, came a group of nine smooth-limbed Korrigans, their red-gold hair tossing on the wind behind them. In the midst of the hanging cradle lay a tiny baby, with widely opened eyes and a solemn pink face, sucking a fat round thumb.

"They have stolen him from his mother, while she dreamt of fairy gold," the Wood-Elf sighed. "She should not have left her door on the latch; it was a sad mistake. In her little one's place there is now a Poupican. At first she will not know, but will fondle and kiss the changeling as if he were her own. After a while she will grieve to find that he gives her no love in return for hers, and plays as readily with strangers as with his mother. But her husband, who is a hard man, will rejoice at the wee child's cleverness. For he will have an old head on young shoulders, and be wise beyond his years."

While the Wood-Elf was speaking, poor Annette's baby lay contentedly beside the crystal goblet, sucking his thumb and looking up at the stars. The Korrigans had left off singing now, and they were passing round the golden cup when there came on the wind the sound of a church bell. Flinging the cup and the goblet into the pond, and staying only to wind the baby in their clinging veils, the Korrigans fled into the darkness with cries of anguish. Some spell seemed to hold me, or I should have tried to rescue the little thing; for it was dreadful to think what might happen to him with the Korrigans.

But the Wood-Elf was quite comforting. "He will be well taken care of," she said, "and someday Annette may break the spell, with the help of the Curé. Rose-Marie got back her child by her own wit, but then she has the name of the blessed Mother. 'You would like to know how?' Then I must speak softly, lest a Korrigan should hear."

Rose Marie and the Poupican.

"Rose-Marie was very young when she married Pierre," began the Elf, "and nothing his mother or hers could say would induce her to beware of Korrigans when her baby came.

'They would not hurt him even if they could,' she cried. 'Who could harm anything so small and sweet?' And she actually set his cradle under the cherry trees, so that his round pink face was covered with fallen petals. Then she went to fetch Pierre from his sowing that he might see how his little son was hidden under the spring snow, and lingered on her way to gather a cluster of purple violets.

When she had disappeared, the Korrigans stole her baby, leaving a Poupican in the fragrant nest. The sun had gone in when she came back, and the little creature was wailing fretfully, Rose-Marie snatched him to her bosom and tried to soothe him, but from that day forward she had no rest. Her milk was sweet and plentiful, and the cradle was soft and warm, but he gave neither her nor her good man Pierre a moment's peace. All through the hours of the night he wailed, and tore at her hair when she held him close to her, scratching her face like an angry kitten.

When he grew older, he was just as bad, for there was no end to his mischief. He shut the cat in a bin of flour, and opened the oven door when Rose-Marie was baking, so that the bread was spoilt. He drove the hens into the brook, and cut the cord which tethered Pierre's white cow, so that she roamed for miles. And with all he did, he never uttered a word. It was this which first roused Rose-Marie's suspicions, and after that she watched him carefully.

One morning she made up her mind to surprise him into speaking, and as he sat beside the hearth, peering at her through his half-closed eyes, she set an egg shell on the fire, and placing in this a spoonful of broth, stirred it carefully with a silver pin. The Poupican was amazed, for it was nearing the dinner hour, and there would be ten to feed. At last he could contain himself no longer.

Rose-Marie and the Poupican

'What are you doing, Mother?' he asked in a strange cracked voice.

'I am preparing a meal for ten,' returned Rose-Marie, without looking round.

'For ten—in an eggshell?' he cried. 'I have seen an egg before a hen; I have seen the acorn before the oak; but never yet saw I folly such as this!' And he fell to cackling like a full farmyard, rocking himself from side to side, and repeating, 'Such folly I never saw!' until even gentle Rose-Marie was moved to anger.

'You have seen too much, my son,' she said, and lifting him up by the scruff of his neck in spite of his struggles, she carried him out of the house. Then, sitting down on a heap of stones beside the brook, she proceeded to whip him soundly. At his first cry of pain a Korrigan appeared, in the shape of an ugly old woman with bleared red eyes and straggling tresses. She was leading a curly-haired boy by the hand, the living image of Pierre. As she released him he flew across the grass to Rose-Marie and hid his face in her skirts.

'Here is thy son!' croaked the Korrigan. 'I have fed him on meal and honey, and he has learnt no evil. Give me my Poupican, and I will go.'

So Rose-Marie gave up the Poupican, and with a thankful heart took her own son home."

"Do you know any more stories?" I asked when the Elf stopped for breath. I didn't want to go back just yet, for it was jolly in the wood, and I could smell violets close by.

"More than I can tell," replied the Elf, "but you shall hear what happened to Peric and Jean."

The Story of Peric and Jean.

"In a beautiful valley not far from here a number of Korrigans were accustomed to gather on summer nights, for the grass was soft as velvet, and the mountains sheltered it from the breeze. None of the peasants dare cross the valley after dark, lest they might be forced to join their revels; for it was known by all that the Korrigans must dance whether they would or not, until some mortal should break the charm that had been laid upon them.

One evening, when the west was aglow with fire, a farmer was sent for to attend the sick bed of his mother, who lived on the other side of the valley. His wife and he had been at work all day in the fields, since labour was scarce and they were poor, and as both loved the old woman dearly, they hurried off without stopping to lay aside their *fourches*—little sticks which are still used in some parts of Brittany as 'plough paddles.' By the time they were half-way across the valley, the dusk had fallen, and they found themselves encircled by angry Korrigans, who shrieked with rage and made as if they would tear them to pieces. Before they had touched them, however, they all fell back, and a moment later broke into singing. This was their song:—

'Lez y, Lez hon,
(*Let him go, let him go,*)
Bas an arer zo gant hook;
(*For he has the wand of the plough;*)
Lez on, Lez y,
(*Let her go, let her go,*)
Bas an arer zo gant y!'
(*For she has the wand of the plough!*)

Then the dancers made way for the farmer and his wife, who reached the old mother safely, and comforted her last hours.

When they returned to their own homes they told what they had seen and heard. Some of the villagers were still too much afraid of the Korrigans to venture, but others armed themselves with *fourches*, and hastened to the valley when night had fallen. All of these witnessed the famous dance, but none felt inclined to join it.

In a neighbouring village two tailors dwelt, and they were as anxious as the rest to see the Korrigans. The elder was a tall and handsome fellow named Jean, but in spite of his inches he had no pluck, and was idle as well as vain. The other was Peric, a red-haired hunchback, so kind and lovable in spite of his looks that if ever a neighbour were in trouble, it was to Peric he went first. Though the hunchback and Jean shared the same business, the latter was always gibing at Peric, and left him to do most of the work.

'Since you're so courageous,' he sneered, one fine warm night when he and Peric had stayed behind in the valley to watch the Korrigans, 'suppose you ask them to let you join their dance. Your hump should make you safe with them, for they are not likely to fall in love with you.'

'All right,' said Peric cheerfully, though at this unkind reference to his deformity his face had flushed. And taking off his cap he approached the whirling Elves.

'May I dance with you?' he asked politely, dropping his *fourche* to show he trusted them.

'You're more brave than good looking,' they replied, their feet still moving to the same quick measure. 'Are you not afraid that we shall work you ill?'

'Not a bit!' answered Peric, joining hands with them; and he started to sing as lustily as they:—

'*Dilun, Dimeurs, Dimerc'her,*'

which means 'Monday, Tuesday, Wednesday.' After a while he grew tired of singing these three words so often, and went on of his own accord:—

'*Ha Diriaou, ha Digwener,*'
(And Thursday and Friday!)

'*Mat! Mat!*' (Good! Good!) cried the Korrigans in chorus, and though he could not tell why they were so delighted, he was glad to have given them pleasure. When they offered him the choice of wealth or power in return for some mysterious service which he seemed to have rendered them, he only laughed, for he thought that they were poking fun at him.

'Take away my hump, then,' he cried at last, 'and make me as handsome as my friend Jean. A little maid whom I love dearly will not look at me when he is near, though she likes well enough to talk to me by the fountain if he is out of the way.'

They tossed him three times in the air.

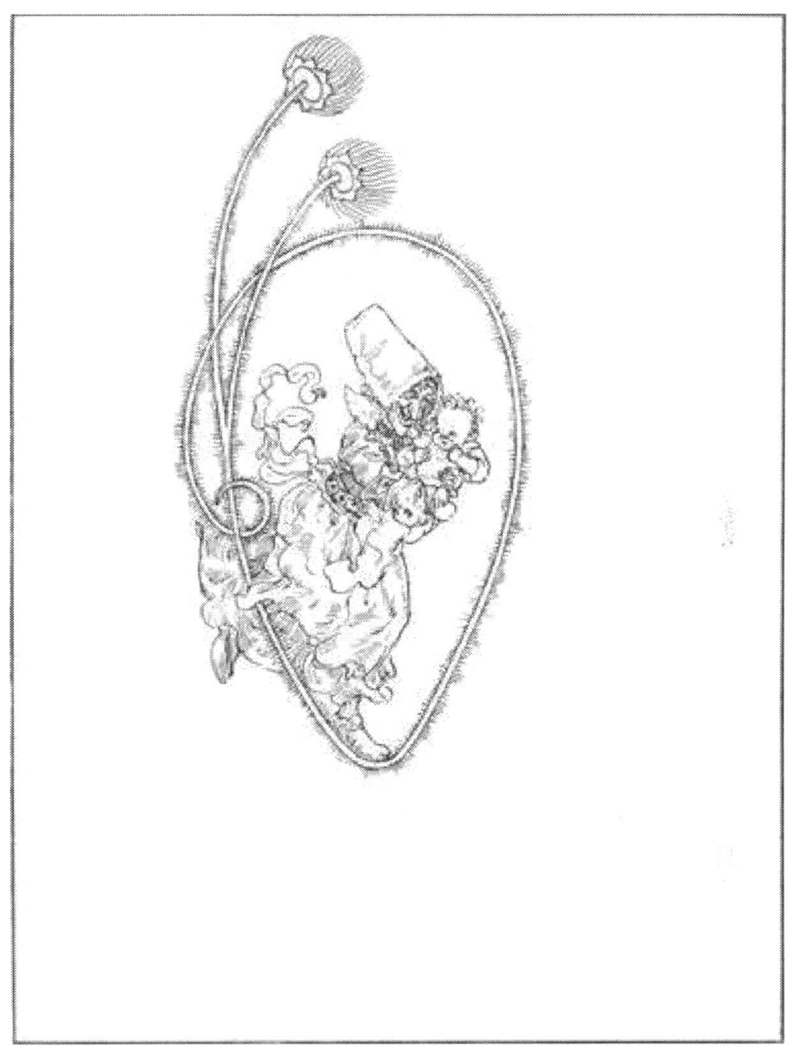

‘Is that all?’ exclaimed the Korrigans. ‘That will not give us the slightest trouble!’ and catching him in their veils, they tossed him three times in the air. The third time he alighted on his feet. He was now as tall and straight as he could wish to be, with fine soft hair as black as the raven’s wing.

Instead of rejoicing at his friend’s good fortune, Jean was full of envy. Forgetting his fears in his greed for gain, he pushed himself into the midst of the Korrigans, who had once more begun to dance, and joined them in their singing. His voice was less melodious than Peric's, and he did not keep time so well, but they suffered him amongst them out of curiosity.

Presently he, like Peric, grew tired of the monotonous chant, and shouted:

'Ha Disadarn, ha Disul'
(And Saturday and Sunday)

'What else? what else?' cried the Korrigans in great excitement, but he only looked as stupid as an owl, and repeated these words over and over. Catching him in their veils, they tossed him up as they had done Peric, and when he came down again he found he had red hair and a hump. They were angry you see, that he had come so near to breaking the spell and had then disappointed them, for if he had only had the sense to add:

'Ha cetu chu er sizun,'
(And now the week is ended)

he would have broken the spell and set them free, since Peric had already sung 'And Saturday and Sunday.'"

There were so many things in Brittany that Father wanted to show me—places he had seen with Mother, and curious monuments, and lovely views,—that I could not get out alone again until the day before we went on to Normandy. No Fairy would ever speak to me unless I was quite by myself, and the quaint little men who peered out from the old ruins when I ran on in front, scampered away at once when Father came in sight.

On that last morning a funny old postman in a blue cap brought him some letters from home. They were about the practice, and Father said that he must stay indoors to answer them. The patients did not seem to like the "locust" at all, according to Nancy. I don't suppose he gave them such nice-tasting medicines as Father did.

The moment he took up his pen I was off to the wood. The paths were carpeted with velvet moss, and starry flowers peeped through the green. Some bees were buzzing round a clump of violets that grew by the side of the fountain, and sitting on the steps were two hideous old women, with bleared red eyes and wisps of faded hair. As I drew near they scowled most horribly, and vanished in the spray. I was delighted to find my Wood-Elf by the violets, for somehow the sight of those two old crones had made me shiver.

"They were Korrigans!" the Wood-Elf whispered. "That is how they look by daylight, so it is no wonder that they hate to be seen by mortals! I shouldn't advise you to come here to-night, for they will bear you a grudge, and might tempt you to dance with them!"

I thought of what had befallen Jean, and shook my head. It must be dreadful to have a hump, though I read of one once that turned into wings. But Jean's didn't seem that kind.

"I know better than to put myself in their power," I cried, and the Wood-Elf laughed.

"You think you are very wise," she said, pausing the next moment to coax a bee to give her a sip of honey, "but mortal men are not a match for Fairy Folk. The Dwarfs, or Courils, who haunt the stone tables and curious mounds you find throughout this country, compel all travellers by night who come their way to dance with them, whether they will or no. They don't let them stop dancing until they drop to the ground, worn out with fatigue, and sometimes the poor creatures never regain their strength. Mère Gautier's husband danced with the Dwarfs when he was but eight-and-twenty, and he has not done a stroke of work from that day to this, though now he is eighty-five. Mère Gautier keeps the home together, and he sits by the fireside and tells the neighbours how the Dwarfs looked and what they said. The Curé declares that such idleness is sinful, and that he might work if he would; but one cannot be sure, and he makes himself out to be a very poor creature.

The Gorics—tiny men but three feet high, though they have the strength of giants—are little better than Courils. Near Quiberon, by the sea shore, is a heap of huge stones, some say no less than four thousand in number, known as 'The House of the Gorics,' and every night the Dwarfs come out and dance round it till break of day. If they spy a belated traveller, even in the distance, they compel him to join them, just as the Courils do; and when he faints from sheer exhaustion they vanish in peals of laughter."

"The Fairy I met in the South spoke of little men who gave away fairy gold," I said, trying not to let my voice sound sleepy. The sun was hot, though it was early spring, and there was a grasshopper just at my elbow who had been chirping a lullaby to her babies for the last half-hour.

"If you shut your eyes you will see nothing!" the Wood-Elf pouted; and I knew that she had noticed my yawn. I sat up then, and told her how pretty I thought her frock, all brown and green, with a dainty girdle of silver. She laughed at this, and I coaxed her to tell me another story. It was one, she said, that had been sung in verse on the Welsh hills, for in ancient times the people of Wales and those of "Little Britain" were the closest friends.

"Long, long ago," she began, "a lordly castle was built at Morlaix, in the midst of such pleasant surroundings that some little Dwarfs in search of a home thought that they could not do better than build their stronghold underneath it. So they set to work immediately, for they have a very wise rule that when once they decide that a thing must be done, it shall be done at once. By the time that the castle was finished, their home was completed too. Far below the ground they had fashioned a number of oval chambers, with ceilings encrusted with gleaming pearls which they found in the bay, and floors paved with precious amber.

The Wee Men of Morlaix

Beyond these chambers lay their treasure house, where they kept rich stores of fairy gold, and the winding passages which led to the upper world were only just wide enough to allow them to creep through. Their entrances were cunningly contrived to look like rabbit holes, so that strangers might think they led to nothing more than some sandy warren.

But the country folk knew better, for they often watched the little men run in and out, beating a faint tattoo on the silver basins in which they collected the morning dew and the evening mist, which served them for food and drink. Now and then, when the sky was a vault of blue, and the sun shone his brightest, they brought up piles of their golden coins, that they might see them glisten in the light of day. So friendly were they to mortals, that if they were surprised while thus employed, they seldom failed to share their wealth.

One very bleak autumn there was much distress on the countryside, for the harvest had failed for the third season, and many of the smaller farmers were on the verge of ruin. Jacques Bosquet—*Bon Jacques*—his neighbours called him, for he had never refused his help to a friend in need—was one of these. His frail old mother was weak and ailing, and he did not know how to tell her that she must leave the homestead to which she had come as a bride, full fifty years before. In his despair he tried to borrow a thousand francs from a rich merchant in the next town; but the merchant was a hard man, and his mouth closed like a cruel steel trap when he told Jacques roughly that he had no money to lend. As Jacques returned home his eyes were so dim with the tears which pride forbade him to shed, that in passing the castle of Morlaix he all but fell over three little men, who were counting out gold by a deep hole.

'What is wrong with you, friend, that you do not see where you are going?' cried the eldest of the three; and when Jacques told them of his fruitless errand, they at once invited him to help himself to their treasure.

'Take all you can hold in your hand!' they urged, and since Jacques' hand had been much broadened with honest toil, this meant a goodly sum. The three little men had vanished before Jacques found words to express his gratitude, and he hurried away with a thankful heart. The coins were of solid gold, and stamped with curious signs; to his great joy he very soon sold them for a big price, and had now sufficient not only to pay his debts, but to carry him through the winter.

When the merchant who had received his appeal so churlishly heard of his good fortune, he was full of envy, and determined to lay in wait for the little men himself. Though blessed with ample means, he coveted more, and when at last he surprised the Dwarfs as Jacques had done, he made so piteous a tale that they generously allowed him to take two handfuls instead of one. But this did not content the greedy fellow, and pushing the wee men rudely away, he stooped to fill his pockets from the heap. As he did so, a shower of blows rained fiercely round his head and face, and so heavily did they fall that he had much ado to save his skull. When at last the blows ceased, and he dared to open his eyes, the Dwarfs had gone, with all their gold, and his pockets were empty of even that which they had contained before."

The Wood Elf paused, for a large brown bird had perched himself on a branch which overhung the fountain. She waited until he had dipped his beak in the sparkling stream and flown away before she spoke again.

"That bird is a stranger to these woods," she said presently under her breath, "and I wondered if it were really an Elf or a Fée. One never knows in these parts."

"Tell me!" I urged; for I knew by her look that she was thinking of another story.

"There was once a most beautiful lady," she began, "whose face was so kind and gentle that wherever she went the children flocked round her and hung on her gown. No flower in the garden could hold up its head beside her, for the roses themselves were not so sweet, and even the lilies drooped before her exceeding fairness.

From far and near lovers came to woo her, but she would none of them; for ever in her mind was a gallant knight to whom she had plighted her troth in the land of dreams. In the presence of a holy man, whose features were those of the Curé who confirmed her, he had placed a ring upon her finger; and so real did this dream seem, that she held herself to to be the knight's true wife.

The Bird at the Window.

Her songs were all of him as she sat at her spinning, and her tender thoughts made warp and weft with the shining threads. When she went to the fountain, she heard his voice in the splash of the falling water, and when the stars shone through her casement, she fancied that they were the adoring eyes of her beloved. She prayed each night that she might be patient and faithful until he claimed her, for he, and none other, should touch her lips.

But she was very beautiful, and her parents were very poor. And when the lord of those parts saw and desired her, they gave her to him, despite her prayers, though he was bent and old. He carried her off to his grim castle, and that no man but he should gaze on her loveliness, he shut her in his tower, with only an aged widow as her attendant. The widow was half-blind and wholly deaf, and withal so crabbed in disposition that as she passed the very dogs in the street slunk off to a safe distance. In vain the beautiful lady pleaded to be allowed to stroll in the gardens, or to ply her needle on the balcony; he would not let her stir from her gloomy chamber, and for seven long years he kept her in durance. His love had by this time turned to hate, for her beauty was dimmed with weeping. No longer did her hair make a mesh of gold for sunbeams to dance in, and her face was like a sad white pearl from which all tints had fled. And the heart of the wicked lord rejoiced, for since he could not win her favour, and she no longer delighted his eyes, he was glad that she should die.

One morning in May when the dew lay thick upon the meadows and every thrush had found a mate, the old lord went off for a long day's hunting, and the aged widow fell fast asleep. The beautiful lady sighed anew as the sweet spring sunshine flooded her prison, seeming to mock her with its splendour. 'Ah, woe is me!' she cried. 'I may not even rejoice in the sun as the meanest of God's creatures!' And in her great despair she called aloud to her own true knight, bidding him deliver her from her misery. Even as she spoke, a shadow fell across the window. A bird had stayed his flight beside it; he pressed through the bars and was at her feet. His ash-brown plumage and rounded wings told her he was a goshawk, and from the jesses on his legs she saw he had been a'hunting. While she gazed in surprise at his sudden appearance, she beheld a transformation, and in less time than it takes to tell, the goshawk had become a gallant knight, with raven locks and flashing eyes. It was the knight of her dreams, and with a cry of joy she flew to him.

'I could not come to thee before, my Sweet,' said he, 'since thou didst not call for me aloud. Now shall I be with thee at thy lightest wish, and no more shalt thou be lonely. But beware of the aged crone who guards thy door! Her purblind eyes are not beyond seeing, and should she discover me I must die.'

And now the beautiful lady no longer pined to leave her prison, for she had only to breathe his name, and her lover reappeared. Her beauty came back to her as gladness to the earth when the sun shines after rain, and her songs were as joyous as those of the lark when it soars high in the heavens. The old lord was greatly puzzled, and bade the ancient widow keep a careful watch.

'My beautiful lady is gay!' he said, with an ugly smile. 'We must learn why she and sighs are strangers. I had thought ere this to lay her to sleep beneath a smooth green coverlet, and it does not please me to see her thus content.'

The aged crone bathed her eyes in water that flowed from a sacred shrine, so that sight might come back to them, and hid herself behind a curtain when the beautiful lady thought that she had left the tower. From this place of vantage she beheld, shortly after, the arrival of the goshawk, and his transformation into a handsome and tender knight. Slipping away unseen, she hastened to her master and told him all, not forgetting to describe the beautiful lady's rapture in her knight's embrace.

The jealous lord was furious with rage, and caused, at dead of night, four sharp steel spikes to be fixed to the bars of the window in the tower. On leaving his love, the goshawk flew past these safely, but when he returned at dusk the next evening, he overlooked them in his eagerness, and was sorely hurt. The beautiful lady hung over her beloved, distraught with grief; all bleeding from his wounds, he sought to comfort her.

'Dear love, I must die!' he murmured faintly, 'but thou shalt shortly bear me a son who will dispel thy sorrows and avenge my fate.' Then he gave her a ring from his finger, telling her that while she wore it neither the old lord nor the widow would remember aught that she would have them forget. He also gave her his jewelled sword, and bade her keep it till the day when Fate should bring her to his tomb, and she should 'learn the story of the dead.' Then, and then only, he commanded, was his son to know what had befallen him.

She hid herself behind a curtain.

The beautiful lady wept anew, and in a passion of grief begged him not to leave her; but once more bidding her a fond farewell, he resumed the form of a goshawk, and flew mournfully away.

It happened as the knight foretold. Neither the widow nor the old lord remembered his coming, and when the beautiful lady's son was born, the old lord was proud and happy. His satisfaction made him somewhat less cruel to the beautiful lady, who lived but for her boy. In cherishing him her grief grew less, but though she had now her freedom, she never ceased to long for the time when her son should know the truth about his father.

The boy grew into a lad, and the lad into a handsome and gallant knight. He was high in favour at court, since none could approach him in chivalry or swordmanship, and many marvelled that one so brave and pure as he could be the son of the old lord, whose advancing years were as evil as those of his youth had been. One day his mother and he were summoned by the King to a great festival, and rather than let them out of his sight, the old lord rose from his bed to go with them. They halted on their way at a rich Abbey, where the Abbot feasted them royally and before they left desired to show them some of the Abbey's splendours. When they had duly admired the exquisite carvings in the chapels, and the golden chalice on the High Altar, he conducted them to a chapter room, where, covered with hangings of finely wrought tapestry, and gorgeous embroideries of blue and silver, was a stately tomb. Tapers in golden vessels burned at its head and feet, and the clouds of incense that filled the air floated from amethyst vessels. It was the tomb, the Abbot said, of 'a noble and most valiant knight,' who had met his death for love's sweet sake, slain by certain mysterious wounds which he bore on his stricken breast.

When the beautiful lady heard this, she knew she had found the resting place of her own true love, and taking his sword from the silken folds of her gown, where she had ever carried it concealed from view, she handed it to the young knight and told him all.

'Fair son, you now have heard,' she said,
'That God hath us to this place led.
It is your father who here doth lie,
Whom this old man slew wrongfully.'

With this she fell dead at her son's feet; and forthwith he drew the sword from its jewelled scabbard, and with one swift blow smote off the old lord's head.

Thus did he avenge the wrongs of his parents, whom he vowed to keep in his remembrance while life should last."

The fruit trees were a-glow with blossom when we reached Normandy, and the pink and white Elves who played hide-and-seek in the boughs were as lovely as Titania. We spent some time at a big farm, where Father had stayed long ago with Mother, and we drove all over the country in the farmer's gig.

One day I woke quite early, when the birds had only just commenced to twitter, and the sky was still rosy with dawn. I threw open my little casement window as wide as it would go, and the air smelt so sweet, and it was all so beautiful, that I longed to be out-of-doors. In the quiet of the early morning the Elves might be abroad, so I slipped on my things and stole down to the orchard. And there, sure enough, were the Elfin hosts.

But though I told them who I was, they were too shy to talk, and scattered the blossom on my upturned face, when I tried to coax them. A fat brown thrush scolded me for disturbing her babies at their breakfast, and fluttered round me, beating her wings, until I moved away, when the Elves seemed to be as pleased as she was, for they wanted to be left to themselves.

On the opposite side of the orchard was a bank of moss, and I strolled across and sat down in a little hollow. The moss was soft as velvet, and through the boughs of a pear tree, laden with bloom, I could see the gate to the farm-yard. A speckled hen was the only creature in sight, and it amused me to watch how daintily she pecked this side and that. All at once there came an excited chorus of "*Cluck-Cluck-Cluck!*" and it seemed as if every fowl in the place were trying to go through the gate. They were led by a fine young cock, with beautifully bright green head feathers. Once he was safely through, he perched himself on an empty pail, and crowed indignantly.

"*Cock-adoodle-do-oo!*" mocked a voice behind him, and a little boy in a red cap gave him a box on the ears which sent him flying.

"That bird thinks twice too much of himself," he grinned, as he ran to me over the grass. "Who am I? Why, *Nain Rouge* of Normandy, first cousin to Puck and Robin Goodfellow across the water."

He had twinkling eyes that were never still, and a roguish face. I knew I was going to like him immensely, so I showed him my new knife and said he might whittle his stick if he'd promise to give it back to me. *Nain Rouge* felt both blades with a small brown finger, and said they were too blunt for him.

"Blunt?" I cried. "Why, they're as sharp as sharp can be! Just see!" But when I tried to show him how sharp they were, neither would cut at all. I was so surprised that I hadn't a word to say, and *Nain Rouge* doubled himself in two with laughter.

"Never mind," he gasped, when he could speak, "I'll make them all right for you." He touched them again, twisting his tongue round the corner of his mouth, and screwing his eyes up comically.

"Now cut!" he said, and when I found they were as sharp as ever, I shut up the blades, and put the knife back into my pocket. I was glad I had left my watch in the house, for *Nain Rouge* might have tried to play tricks with that.

"Another name I go by is the 'Lutin,'" he said, throwing himself on the ground beside me. "When I have nothing better to do, I *lutine*, or twist, the horses' manes. One summer afternoon two lazy maids fell fast asleep in the hay loft, when they ought to have been down with the reapers in the long field. I *lutined* their hair so nicely for them that when they woke they could not untwist it, and had to cut it off! The House Spirits made rather a fuss, for those girls were pets of theirs, but Abundia, Queen of the Fées and Lutins, said I had done quite right. We can't bear laziness, you know, for we're always busy ourselves."

"What do you do besides mischief?" I said slyly, as he smoothed the feather in his pretty cap. *Nain Rouge* looked quite offended.

"If the truth were told," he said in a huff, "I should fancy I'm twice as much use as you are. The farmers couldn't get on without me. I look after the horses, and help to rub the poor beasts down when they come home tired at the end of the day; I stir their food so that it agrees with them, and scare off the grey goblins who might put it into their heads to work no more at the plough. And I'm as good to the farmers' wives as an extra maid, even if I do take my pay in a drink of cream. I dance my shadow on the wall to amuse the children if they are fretful, and tell them stories when the wind moans down the chimney and would frighten them if it could. And I pinch their toes when they are naughty, and hide the playthings they leave about."

He looked so much in earnest while he told me all this, and so very good, that I was beginning to think he was not half so mischievous as Puck, when he gave a funny little chuckle, and rubbed his hands.

"Such fun as I have with the fishermen!" he cried. "If they forget to cross themselves with holy water before they go to sea, I fill their nets with heavy stones, or entice away the fish. When the fancy takes me, I change myself into the form of a handsome young man, and if folks do not then treat me with proper respect, and call me '*Bon Garçon*' civilly, I pelt them with stones until they run! Their wives and daughters are always gentle to poor *Nain Rouge*, however; and when I can, I do them a good turn. Shall I tell you how I consoled the fair Marguerite when she wept? Then listen well!"

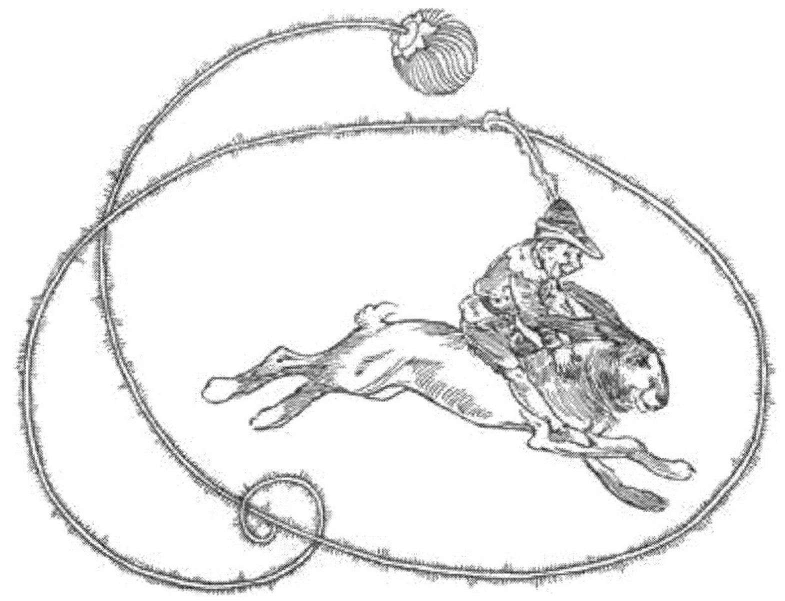

The white Stone of Happiness.

"A favourite haunt of mine," began *Nain Rouge*, "is a little fishing village, close to Dieppe. The maidens there are more to my mind than those on any other part of the coast; their skin is like clear pale amber, warmed into redness where the sun has kissed it, and their eyes—ah! you should see them! The fairest of all was Marguerite, and often I sat for hours on her window-sill to watch her at her spinning. Etienne would come and watch her too, and he thought, foolish lad, that her angel-face meant an angel temper; but I knew she had a tongue.

And such a tongue! It was like the brook, for it never stopped, and she said such sharp and bitter things that the love of her friends withered up as they heard them, just as spring lilies droop before a cruel East wind. Etienne was a stranger, or he would have known better than to woo her seriously. Strange to relate, the wayward maid was different from the day he came. I had never known her so soft and sweet, and the neighbours said that surely some good fairy had laid her under a spell.

Etienne and she were wed one summer morning, but the little new moon had not shone in the heavens a second time when there was trouble between them. Marguerite's tongue was sharper than ever from its long rest, and Etienne could not believe it belonged to his 'angel' bride. He left the cottage without a word, and when he came back his mouth was grim, for his mates had hastened to make things worse by telling him many tales. A foolish man was Etienne, or he would not have heeded them; but that is neither here nor there.

From this time on he made as though he were deaf when Marguerite railed at him, and he took her no more to his breast when he came back from the sea. And Marguerite grieved, for she loved him well in her woman's way, and longed for his caresses. The sight of his pale set face, and his sombre eyes—they were like the eyes of a dog in pain, when the hand he loves best has struck him—stung her to fresh taunts, and there came a day when he answered her back in the same way, and all but struck her. Ah! a woman's tongue can do rare mischief! His mother had never heard an ugly word from him.

One eve I met Marguerite on the shore. She was sobbing bitterly, for she had just come out of a cave in the rocks, where dwelt a Witch who could read the future.

I had taken the form of a slim, dark, serious looking lad, and laying a gentle hand upon her arm, 'What ails you, Madame Marguerite?' I said. She glanced at me piteously, as one who seeks a refuge and knows not where to turn, and wrung her hands.

'I have lost my Etienne's heart for ever, for ever,' she wailed, 'unless I can find the White Stone of Happiness, which a mermaid throws from the depths of the sea once in a thousand years. I may search for months, and never find it; and Etienne holds aloof from me, and grows further away each day.'

Now just at her feet lay a small white stone, smooth and round as a Fairy's plaything. I picked it up and showed it to her.

'It shall be yours,' I told her gravely, 'if you give me your solemn promise to heed my words.'

"What ails you, Madame Marguerite?"

'I promise!' she answered fervently, and the wind tossed her unbound hair until it floated round her shoulders like a Kelpie's mane. A seventh wave rushed up to her feet, and as she moved nearer the breakwater, I sang her this little song:

'Fairy stone of fairy spell,
Marguerite, O guard it well!
When thine anger doth arise
Elves would rob thee of thy prize.
Press it 'neath thy tongue so red,
Hold it firm till wrath has sped.
Smile, speak softly, and behold,
Love shall warm thee as of old.'

Then I gave her the stone, and she clasped it against her bosom and sped to her home.

When Etienne returned he was in a bitter mood. Luck had been against him; he had caught no fish, and his largest net had been torn on the rocks. Marguerite set a meal before him, but he pushed it angrily away; for the broth had burned while she was with the Witch, and tasted anything but pleasant.

'Such food is not fit for a dog!' he cried. "Twas an ill day for me when I came to *Le Pollet!* I had done better to drown myself.'

Marguerite stayed her fierce reply that she might slip the white stone between her lips; and as she held it beneath her tongue her anger suddenly melted. She thought now of Etienne's hunger and weariness, and was sorry that she had nought in the house for him to eat. And as he sat in moody silence she stole away, and begged some good broth from her godmother, who had always enough and to spare. This she placed before him beside the hearth, and smiled, and spoke in a gentle voice that made him turn to her with a start—it was just as if the Marguerite he loved had come back to him from the grave. Then he drew her to him, hiding his face in her dress; and for the first time since many a long day there was peace between them. Marguerite kept that white stone always, and when she was tempted to speak in anger it worked like a Fairy spell."

"And wasn't it one?" I asked, as *Nain Rouge* put on his cap again, and a delicious smell of fried eggs and bacon came from the farmhouse kitchen on the breeze.

"Not it," said *Nain Rouge*, laughing heartily, "there were thousands like it on the beach, but you see it did just as well. For if once a woman can be induced to hold her tongue when she is angry, there'll be little trouble 'twixt man and wife. This has been so from all time."

"*Cock-a-doodle doo!*" cried the black cock, strutting grandly in front of us. *Nain Rouge* darted after him, and I left them to themselves and went in to breakfast.

I did not see *Nain Rouge* again, but I heard a great deal about him from Madame Daudet, the farmer's wife; she called him "the plague of her life." She said he hid her spectacles every time that she laid them down, and that it was quite impossible to make good butter, for he would play tricks with the cream. I think she was fond of him, all the same, for when I mentioned his name her jolly old face crinkled up into smiles, and she looked quite pleased and happy.

One day when Father had gone to the village to see some sick child whom the peasants believed to have been gazed at with "an evil eye," because it seemed unable to get well, Madame came to me as I stood prodding with a stick some fat black pigs who would not stir.

"Since you are so fond of Fairy Folk," she said, "why not go to the valley, and see if you can meet a Fée? I have never seen one myself, but my great-great-grandmother came across a bevy of them in a forest near Bayeux. The loveliest one was their Queen, and my great-great-grandmother talked of her beauty until her dying day."

"All right," I said. And she gave me some brown bread and a golden apple, so that I need not come home for tea. Perhaps she wanted to get me out of the way, for the sick child's aunt was coming to pay her a visit, and she liked a gossip.

The valley was very still. Even the birds seemed to have gone to sleep, and the stream that trickled down from the hill tinkled very softly, as if it had to be careful not to wake the ferns that fringed its banks. As I looked up the glade I saw a lovely little lady coming slowly towards me, and my heart began to thump in the queerest way. She wore a trailing silvery gown, with a deep band of blue at its border. Her shoes were set with tiny diamonds, and her dainty feet moved through the grass as prettily and as softly as the wind does through the corn. She did not see me until she had come quite close, for I stood in the shade of a blossoming bush. As I took off my cap, her fair face flushed deeply, and for a moment I feared she would run away. So I hastened to tell her that I was a Christmas Child, and why I had come to the valley. At this she smiled, and I saw that her eyes were as blue as the depths of the sea.

"You are welcome," she said, "though at first I feared you. Such sorrow has come to Fées through mortals that we are wont to fly at man's approach. But a Christmas Child is almost a Fée himself, and I may talk to you. My name is Méllisande."

Then she asked me to walk with her through the wood, and I felt quite proud when she took my hand. A cheeky little Elf, who overheard me say that I would go with her anywhere, turned a somersault in the air and burst out laughing, but I pretended not to hear. It wasn't his business, anyhow, and I wished that that walk through the valley had been twice as long.

At the further end, quite hidden among the larches, was a natural grotto of moss-grown stones, and just inside it a heap of ferns, piled up to make a throne that was fit for a queen. Méllisande seated herself on this, and I sat down at her feet.

We did not talk for a long while, for she seemed to be thinking as she stroked my hair, and I only wanted to look at her. After awhile I asked her if she had been one of the Fées that Madame Daudet's great-great-grandmother had met in a forest near Bayeux. She smiled and sighed as she told me "Yes," and a wood dove flew out of the trees and perched on her shoulder.

"Once upon a time," said Méllisande, "there dwelt at the Castle of Argouges a noble lord who was famous not only for his bravery, but for the extreme beauty of his dark features and slender form. All women loved him, but though he served them with chivalry, as became a knight, he sought his pleasure in the woods and fields rather than in their company. He knew what the brook was humming as it gurgled over the stones, and the wind told him all its secrets as it rustled among the pines. Sometimes he wrote these things on a sheet of paper and read them to himself aloud as he lay on the green sward. The Fées in the forest drew near to listen, for the voice of this lord of Argouges was sweet as the lute of Orpheus, and their lovely Queen lost her heart to him. Day after day she hovered by his side, sighing when he was sad, and rejoicing when the words he sought came quickly to his pen.

Once when he looked up suddenly he saw her as in a vision. A silvery veil of misty gauze half hid her exquisite form; and out of this her face looked down upon him, pure as an angel's, but with the love of a woman in her lustrous eyes. As he sprang to his feet, she melted away in a white cloud, and close to his ear he heard a mournful sigh, as if her spirit grieved to part from his. And he wrote no longer of flowing water or whispering wind, but of the Lady of the Woods.

For many a day he saw her no more, for Henry I of England coveted Normandy, the ancient patrimony of his house, and sent his armies to take possession of it. When the city of Bayeux was besieged, the Lord of Argouges was amongst its most gallant defenders, and his resource and daring were the talk of all. None who crossed swords with him lived to tell the tale, for his courage was equalled by his skill.

One morn a giant sprang from the enemy's ranks—a lusty German, well over seven feet, with the limbs of a prize-fed ox.

'I dare you to fight me singly, Lord of Argouges!' he cried, for he knew with whom he had to deal. The soldiers near stayed their hands to watch; the hearts of the Normans almost stood still, but the English exulted, for surely now would the Lord of Argouges bite the dust, and his fiery sword no more work havoc in their ranks! Their dismay was great when he proved himself victor, though they would not have wondered had they had vision to see how ever beside him moved the shadowy form of his Lady of the Woods, directing his arm that his aim might be swift and sure, and oft-times interposing her tender body between him and the German's thrusts. Later on, when the gallant knight fainted from his wounds and was left for dead, she tended him pitifully as he lay on the blood-stained earth, moistening his lips with the dew of heaven, and whispering such sweet thoughts to him that the weary hours were eased by blissful dreams. He was still alive when morning dawned, and was found by his friends and carried into camp. Though visible to him alone, the Lady of the Woods was there beside his couch, and the terrible sights and sounds that accompanied the merciful efforts of those who tended the wounded could not scare her away from him. When his suffering was over, and he could raise himself to eat and drink, she came to him no more, and as his strength slowly returned he was consumed with a passionate desire to find her.

At length he was able to go home to his castle, and once more he roamed the forest. The songs of the birds were hushed by now, and the trees under which he used to rest were almost bare. It was autumn, for he had been long absent, and even yet his step was slow and his proud head bent with weakness. He was sick with longing for his gentle lady; 'If I do not find her, I shall die!' he cried.

Presently he came to a glade where the naked boughs formed a splendid arch above his head, and he saw a troop of horsewomen riding toward him on snow-white steeds. In their midst was his Lady of the Woods, a bridal veil on her star-crowned hair, and myrtle at her breast. He awaited her approach in a trance of delight; nearer and nearer came the prancing horses, their skins of satin glinting in the sun. The cavalcade reached his side; the Queen of the Fées dismounted and stood beside him, while the ground at her feet became a bed of lilies. The Lord of Argouges threw himself on his knees amidst their fragrance, gazing up at her with enraptured eyes, as softly and shyly she bent toward him.

“The Lord of Argouges threw himself on his knees”

‘Once more I greet you, dear lord!’ she said, and as she touched his forehead with her lips, the birds still lingering in the forest burst into joyful song. When the knight found words to tell her of his great love, she plighted her troth to him, but only he heard her whispered promise that she would be his wife.

Once more she mounted her snow-white steed; he seated himself behind her, and thus they rode to the castle gates, accompanied by her maidens. Here the Lord of Argouges sprang to the ground; light as a wisp of thistledown, she floated into his arms, and to the amaze of the household, who had watched the approach of the procession from the castle windows, her horse, thrice neighing, changed into a bird, and fluttered sorrowfully away.

'Farewell, sweet Queen!' her maidens cried, and kissing their hands to her, rode swiftly back to the depths of the forest.

Then the Lord of the Argouges drew the Lady of the Woods across the threshold of the castle, and so queenly was her beauty and so gracious her demeanour, that even his aged mother, jealous of the son for whom she would have shed her life-blood, found no word to say against his choice.

'My love for him is nought beside thine,' the Fée Queen pleaded very sweetly, 'for thou didst bring him into the world, and hast anguished for him as none else can. But I too have suffered on his behalf; I pray thee, let me love him too!'

Then his mother looked long and deeply into the eyes of the woman who had dethroned her from her dear son's heart, and what she saw there filled her with peace. 'Be it as thou wilt,' she said, and that self-same night the Lord of Argouges wedded his Lady of the Woods in the castle chapel, which was decked with the fragrant lilies that sprang wherever her feet had trod. The rejoicings lasted for seven days, and the Lord of Argouges looked as one to whom the gates of Paradise had opened.

The Queen of the Fées was now to all seeming a mortal woman, and so far from regretting that she had laid aside her rank, each day found her more content in her husband's love, and by every womanly art she knew she sought to please him. One favour only she asked of him—that never in her hearing would he mention the word 'Death.'

'If you do, you will lose me for ever,' she told him fearfully, and he vowed by all that he held most sacred that this dread word should not cross his lips.

The years went on. The lovely Lady of the Woods bore him fair daughters and gallant sons, and all was well with the Lord of

Argouges. But one thing grieved him; since the Fées' sweet Queen had linked her lot with his, she too was subject to the laws of Time, and her beauty waned with increasing age. The gold of her hair was streaked with silver, and her face lost some of its soft pink bloom. Her lord spake no word of what was in his mind as he looked at her earnestly one bright spring morn, but she divined his regretful thoughts, and full sorrowful were her own.

The Fées could not help her, since she had left her fairy kindred to throw in her lot with mortal man, and so, with woman's wit, she determined that at the forthcoming festival at the Court the splendour of her attire should make her lord forget Time's changes. She therefore summoned to the castle the most skilful workers in silks and broideries, who toiled in her service day and night, that she might be richly adorned at the Royal Tournament.

Her gown was of azure satin, encrusted with many gems, and her long court train glittered and shone with gold and silver. Diamonds blazed at her breast and neck, while a circlet of rubies glowed in her hair. But their rich red lustre made her pale sweet face look paler than ever, and she still gazed wistfully at her glass though the Lord of Argouges waited below, wondering what delayed her. At length he sought her himself, and in spite of his impatience, he could but admire her resplendent attire.

'You have robbed the sky of his morning glories!' he told her gallantly. Then, as she lingered still, his impatience returned: 'Fair spouse,' he said, 'it were well if Death should send you as his messenger, for you tarry long when you are bidden to haste!—Forgive me, Sweet! I should not have said that word!'

His remorse came too late, for the ominous sound had scarcely crossed his lips when with a cry of bitter anguish, his lady became once more a Fée, and vanished from his sight. Long and vainly did he seek her, for though her footmarks are still to be seen on the battlements of the Castle, and night after night she wandered round it clad in a misty robe of white, they two met on earth no more. She is pictured still in the crest of the house of Argouges, over its motto, 'A la Fe!'"

I liked this story, but I wished that it had not ended quite so sadly. When I said so to Méllisande she turned her face away from me, and I think it was a tear drop that glittered on her hand.

"Then I will tell you neither of Pressina nor Melusina," she said, "for both these Fées lived to rue the day when they put faith in the word of man. It was different with the fair Norina. She demanded no pledge, for doubt and distrust came not nigh her path, and her love brought her only gladness."

The shadows lengthened; the wood dove flew off to rejoin her mate; and Méllisande's lips began to smile as she thought of another story.

"Long, long ago," she went on presently, "when our beautiful Normandy was known by another name, and formed part of the kingdom of Neustria, which was given to the Duke of Paris by Charles the Bald, there lived a wise and noble lord who was said to have magic powers. So gentle was he that the very birds would perch on his shoulder and twitter their joys to him, yet so brave and strong that the proudest knight cared not to provoke his wrath. He was skilled in the lore of plants and herbs, and by means of a slender hazel from the woods could tell where crystal waters flowed deep in the bowels of the earth.

The Seven Fair Queens of Pirou.

Full many a maid would have flown to him had he lifted his little finger, but though he was often lonely as he wandered beneath the stars, his heart went out to none, whether of high or low degree, and he preferred his own company to that of a mate whom he could not love.

One Mayday he was up at dawn, searching the fields for a tiny plant which had some special gift of healing. The grass was spangled with myriad flowers, but he passed them all till he came to the one he sought—a small pale blossom of faintest lilac, with perfume as sweet as a rose's. While yet he held it in his hand he heard a cry; it was that of some creature in pain, and forcing his way through a prickly hedge, he found a pure white dove with a broken wing lying under a thornbush.

'Poor bird!' he exclaimed compassionately. 'Who has dared to injure so fair a thing?' With tender hands he set the broken wing, binding it to her side with three green leaves and some long-stemmed grass, and fed her with juice from the lilac flower as he soothed her with gentle words. When he had stilled her flutterings, he laid her on his breast, that he might bear her home and tend her until she could fly once more under the vault of heaven.

On he strode through the meadow, and high in the sky the larks trilled their pæans of joy. Never to him had seemed the earth so fair, and the morning sun tinged his cheek with gladness. Suddenly he felt the burden on his breast grow heavy, and stayed his footsteps in surprise. No longer did he hold a wounded dove against his bosom, but a beauteous maiden in pure white garb, with three green leaves bound about her arm with stems of grass.

He set her on her feet and stared at her in amaze; she met his enraptured gaze with eyes that shone like twin blue stars. Then her eyelids fell; she drooped beneath his glance as a fragile flower beneath the sun's fierce wooing.

And as the wind sweeps over a field of corn when it is ripe for reaping, love took possession of him. Fée or woman, he swore, this beauteous maid should be his wife if she were willing, and he would guard her through good and ill while life should last.

'Art thou mine?' he asked her presently, hoarse for very joy.

'I am thine!' she said, for she had loved him long, and had but taken the form of a dove to try him. And taking her home to his castle, they were wedded by the holy priest.

No longer now was he lonely, no longer did he wander solitary beneath the stars, for the lovely Fée was as true and tender as mortal woman, and made him a faithful wife. Sons were denied them, but seven fair daughters came, and he called them after the seven gems that graced their mother's diadem.

The maidens were of such supreme loveliness that as they grew up to womanhood they were known as the Seven Fair Queens; each was without rival in her own style of beauty. Pearl was fair as day, with a skin like milk; Ruby's dark splendour was a gift from the Queen of Night, and her red, red mouth the bud of a perfect flower. The glorious hair of Amber fell round her shoulders in shimmering waves of light, and sunbeams lost themselves in her lashes. Sweet Turquoise had her mother's eyes of blue forget-me-not, while Sapphire's were of deeper hue, and Amethyst's that of the violet. Chrysolite's were a misty green, like the sky in the early morning, and no mermaid sang sweeter songs than she as she sat on the rocks at low tide.

There came a time when the father of the Seven Fair Queens fell very sick, and not all his potions could prolong his days. His call had come, and so closely were he and Norina united, that one eve at sunset her life went out with his. For awhile their orphaned daughters wept with grief as they paced the gardens, or sat by the crackling fire in the great hall. But youth cannot mourn for ever, and with a second spring, glad hopes came back to them, and once more they rode in the chase. Since they were rich as well as beautiful you may be sure they had many wooers, but all preferred to reign alone.

'When we wed, it will be with Fées!' they said disdainfully. This angered their lovers, and presently they were left in peace.

Full wisely did they use their parents' wealth, improving the land and making sure provision for all dependant on their bounty. On the coast of the Cotentin they built the Castle of Pirou, which gave work to the poor for several succeeding years, and when it was finished they filled it with gorgeous tapestries and all the treasures of art they could collect. Here they lived in splendour, keeping open house; no passing wayfarer, however humble, need miss a welcome if he cared to claim it.

They were still in the first full bloom of their beauty when their fame reached the ears of one of the great sea pirates, the dreaded Vikings who rode the waves like giant birds of prey. North, South, East and West, from Norway and Sweden, and little Denmark, they sailed in search of plunder, and such was their love of fighting that they would, if need be, challenge each other rather than allow their swords to rust with disuse. Although they robbed, they were brave men, and believed themselves entitled to all they took. Their vessels were small, and light of draught, so they could penetrate many rivers, but the great chiefs chose the sea for their battle ground, and ravaged many a town and village on the coast of France.

When the mighty Siegmund heard of the Seven Fair Queens of Pirou, he resolved to storm their castle and take the loveliest for his bride. With this intent he set sail for the coast of Cotentin with a gallant fleet. The wind and the tide were with him; he reached it one soft spring morning when the sea was a sheet of blue.

As the vessel which bore him neared the shore, the Viking espied a bevy of maidens in a sheltered cove, where the sand lay in golden ripples. Ruby and Pearl, and the gentle Turquoise sported in a sun-kissed pool; while Sapphire and Amethyst wove wreaths of seaweed, and Amber was smoothing her shining hair with a slender shell of mother-of-pearl that the waves had thrown at her feet. Chrysolite sat on a dark rock, singing, and her soft clear notes rang over the waters, enchanting Siegmund with their music.

'By Thor and Odin,' he thundered, 'our journey was well planned. Haste thee, my men, and get me to that rock! That maiden shall be my bride.'

The boat sped swiftly, with Siegmund sitting in the stern. His yellow locks streamed over his stalwart shoulders, and his face was like that of some eager god as he noted Chrysolite's beauty. The maiden saw his approach; and now the glad notes of her exquisite song changed to a mournful rhythm. She was chanting the words that her mother had breathed to her seven daughters as she lay a'dying:

'Women ye, my daughters fair
(Cloudless spreads the sky);
But when menace fills the air,

Fées, as once was I.
Slender arm shall change that day
Into snow-white plume;
Winged as birds, haste swift away
From thy threatening doom!'

"They instantly changed into snow-white birds."

As the last words left her sorrowful lips, Chrysolite's sisters gathered round her; the boat's keel grated on the sand, and Siegmund sprang eagerly forward. At the same moment the Seven Fair Queens of Pirou raised their arms, and instantly these changed, before his eyes, to fluttering wings. High in the air mounted the maidens, and to the bewildered gaze of Siegmund they were nought but a line of snow-white birds flying westward in single file high up in the sky.

When Siegmund had somewhat recovered from his amazement, he and his followers sacked the castle, and pillaged the surrounding country; it did them but little good, for a storm blew up as they sailed back northward, and the ships that carried the stolen treasure were wrecked on the rocks. As for the Seven

Fair Queens, they mated with Fées, and were glad as the morning. Every year as spring comes round, they return to Pirou with their numerous descendants, in the form of a flock of wild geese, and take possession of the nests which they have hollowed out in the crumbling walls. They also appear when a child is born to the house of Pirou; if it be a daughter, and Fate has destined her for a nun, one sits apart in a corner of the courtyard, and sighs as if in sore distress. If a son is born, the male birds display their plumage, and show by their mien that they rejoice."

Méllisande rose from her throne of ferns, "It will be twilight soon," she said, "and we must go. See! the mists are already rising in the valley, and the night-birds awake and call. Farewell, dear Christmas Child, farewell!"

And, stooping down, she kissed my forehead.

Now I knew that Germany was the very country for Dwarfs and Fairies, and when I heard that this was where we were going next I determined to be on the look out. I did not see them, though, for a long time after we arrived, for I was so tremendously interested in everything else. Even in the big cities where Father spent hours and hours in the hospitals, watching the wonderful things that the German doctors did, most of the children looked plump and rosy, and I didn't see any so thin and pale as those we had left at home. One of the Herr Professors, with whom we stayed, said that this was because the State made so kind a Grandmother, but when I asked him what he meant, he only laughed.

I liked this professor best of all—he had such a nice way of talking, and he loved Fairies as much as I do. He said "*Ach! So!*" when I told him I was a Christmas Child, and smiled all over his kind old face. Then he put his hand on my shoulder, and told me that I must remember to do my part to make my birthday the gladdest day in the year for everyone around me.

"It is different in your country," he went on, "but here, in the Fatherland, there is scarcely a cottage home which has not its Christmas tree, even if this is only a branch of fir stuck in a broken pot, and hung with oranges and golden balls. No child is so poor but has his Christmas presents of cakes and toys, for if his mother cannot provide them, she tells his teacher in good time, and the teacher sees that he is not forgotten."

I thought this was a ripping plan, for it is horrid when Santa Claus forgets you, and your stockings hang all limp and flat, like mine did last year. And I made up my mind, then and there, that next Christmas there should be a tree for all the littlest and grubbiest children in my old home.

While Father was at the hospitals with the Herr Professor, I stayed with Rudolf and Gretchen, two of his grandchildren—fat little things with big blue eyes, who stared at me as if I had seven heads when I told them about the Korrigans. Gretchen believed in Fairies of all kinds, but Rudolf only in Dwarfs and Giants. He even said that Santa Claus was just his own father dressed up, and declared he had seen his old brown pipe peeping out of Santa Claus' pocket the last time he paid them a visit.

Fat little things, with big blue eyes.

Gretchen said that if so, Santa Claus had taken away the old brown pipe to bring a lovely new one in its place, and Rudolf told her girls knew too much. They were both angry by this time, and their faces looked very red. So I thought we had better talk about Dwarfs and Giants.

"Grandfather says there are no Giants now," Rudolph said seriously, "but there are plenty of Dwarfs in the hill which looks down on the forest. I saw one there myself last summer; he ran away and wouldn't speak to me, as if he were afraid."

Without saying anything to Rudolf, who might have wanted to come too, I started for the hill directly after dinner, while he and Gretchen were arguing again over the pipe and Santa Claus. The Professor's house was just at the end of the town, so I didn't have far to go; but the hill took much longer to climb than I thought it would, and I was quite out of breath when I reached the top and sat down on a flat white stone. As I looked about me, I swung my foot, and it tapped against a biggish rock that was just in front. The third time that I did this, a little brown man hopped briskly out of a crevice and stood before me. He wore a bright red coat trimmed with green buttons, and carried in his hand a close-fitting cap of grey.

"Gently, gently, good child!" he cried. "One knock is enough, if we want to hear it, for our ears are as keen as we could wish. Why did you call me, and what would you have?"

"I would hear of you, and of your kinsmen, Master Dwarf!" I said. "I am a Christmas Child, and the Fairies are all my friends."

At this he bowed, and said he was glad to meet me, nodding his head with a sort of grunt as I told him where I had met Titania.

"If it be your pleasure," he said, looking round to see that no one was near but me, "I will take you within the hill, and introduce you to my wife. The ground whereon you stand is hollow, as you will soon perceive, and we are less than a stone's throw from my palace."

I told him that nothing would please me more than to pay him a visit, and muttering a word in some strange language, he rapped his knuckles on a cleft in the rock. It widened sufficiently to let us both through, and closed again with a thud.

The winding passage in which I found myself was lit by a soft red glow, coming from hundreds of rubies set deep in the walls, which seemed to be of oxidised silver. After several twists and turns, it ended in a wide hall, where I could just stand upright under the jewelled dome! As soon as my eyes grew accustomed to the blaze of light which came from the diamond stars set round it, I saw a sweet little creature in a frock of pale purple silk, cut short in the sleeves to show her pretty white arms, on which she wore many bracelets.

"My wife!" said the Dwarf proudly, and he explained to her who I was and what I wanted, and a great deal more about me that I was astonished he should know. My surprise amused him a good deal, and as his wife led the way to her boudoir he chuckled merrily.

"There are Kobolds, or House-Spirits in most old houses," he remarked, "and it is more than two hundred years since the first stone was laid of the Herr Professor's. I knew this noon that you were coming, and the Kobold spoke well of you, and said that you were not above taking advice from others wiser than yourself. Now, sir! What do you think of this?" And he opened a door with a great flourish, holding it back for me to enter.

"It's grand!" I said, for so it was. The silver floor was inlaid with a gold scroll; the walls, of tinted mother-o'-pearl, were adorned with wreaths of forget-me-nots, each tiny turquoise flower having an amber centre. The furniture was of filigree silver, so fragile to look at that I was afraid to touch it, much less to sit down on one of the tiny chairs, even if I could have fitted myself in. The Dwarf invited me to be seated, and his small wife gave me a roguish smile as she brought a velvet cushion from an inner room, and placed this on the ground. I found afterwards that it was the Dwarfs own bed, and that his pillow was made of spun spider silk, filled with scented roseleaves and wild thyme.

"When you are rested and refreshed," said the Dwarf kindly, as his little spouse offered me a sip of nectar from a crystal goblet, "I will show you my palace. There is not much to see, for we are humble folk, and this hill comparatively a small one. The estates of some of our nobles extend for miles, and that of our Emperor runs through a range of mountains. In times gone by we welcomed mortals as our guests, for we were anxious to be their friends. But they grudged us even a handful of peas in return, and met our advances with jeers. Now we keep to our hills as far as possible, and when we desire to walk abroad, we are careful to wear our mist caps, which render us quite invisible."

The Dwarf invited me to be seated.

He sighed so deeply that the dainty lace cap poised on his wee wife's hair was almost blown away, and then, straightening his bent shoulders, he took me to see his Banquet Hall. The curtains were all of filigree silver, fine as lace, and on the walls of the kitchen, where silent little men in big white aprons kneaded cakes on crystal slabs, shone ruby and sapphire butterflies.

But this was nothing to what I saw in the long low vault where the Dwarf kept his treasures. At one end was a shimmering heap of pearls, some larger than pigeons' eggs; at another, a conical mound of diamonds, which threw out marvellous lights as the Dwarf stirred them gently with one small hand.

"We know the properties of each stone," he said; "how some give strength, and some wisdom and power to rule, while others still stir up strife and envy, and make men merciless as beasts of prey. That ruby you see has an evil history; a woman gave her soul for it, and thousands were slain in her cause."

I picked up the beautiful, glowing gem, and fancied I saw the face of an evil demon grinning at me from its depths. Dropping it quickly, I looked instead at a pile of rings at the other side of the vault. One in particular drew my attention; it was of beaten gold, with a curious stone set deep in its centre. As I held it aloof and stared at it, I caught a glimpse of a waving meadow, with a tiny path leading past a brook.

"That is the ring which the Queen of Lombardy gave to her son, Otnit," said the Dwarf. "Come with me to the Court of Rest, and you shall hear the story."

This was the loveliest place which I had yet seen in the palace. A circle of orange trees in full bloom enclosed a space round a rippling fountain, where from the gleaming beak of an opal bird a stream of water splashed into an emerald basin. The invisible wind that stirred the petals of the orange blossom brought with it the swish of the sea, and somewhere, far off, a nightingale was singing.

The Dwarf seated himself on one of the velvet cushions strewn on the ground, and motioning me to take another, began his tale.

Dwarf Elberich and the Emperor.

"Otnit, Emperor of Lombardy, was one of the greatest kings that ever lived. By force of wisdom more than by might, he subdued the surrounding nations, and his people looked up to him as to a god. When the time came for him to wed, no maid in his wide dominions pleased his fancy, for the wife he pictured in his dreams was sweet and simple, though of royal birth, and quite unspoiled by praise and flattery. He told his ministers this, and they shrugged their shoulders.

'His Majesty desires the impossible!' they whispered amongst themselves, and so it seemed until the Emperor's Uncle Elias, the wild-bearded King of the Russians, told him of a highborn maid who was as good as she was beautiful, and had never yet been wooed by man.

'She shines o'er other women as bright roses do!' he cried, and Otnit vowed to win her.

On the eve of his departure for Syria, where she dwelt with her father the Soldan, Otnit's mother gave him the ring you held, bidding him take his horse and ride toward Rome while gazing at the gem in the ring, that what he saw there might direct his path. The Emperor smiled, but wishing to humour her, did as she requested, and rode through the silver starlight thinking of his fair maid. At early dawn, when the welkin rang with the song of birds, he saw mirrored in the ring a narrow pathway trodden in the green grass. Making his way by this fragrant road, he reached a linden tree by a lake. Here he stayed his courser, and sprang to the ground, peering beneath its boughs.

'Never yet from tree came so sweet-breathing a wind,' he laughed; for lo! an infant lay on the grass, his fair white frock fringed with many gems. Otnit found it all he could do to lift him, in spite of his strength, but placing the little creature on the saddle, declared his intention of taking him to the palace, and putting him in his mother's care.

But this did not please Dwarf Elberich, who for his own purpose had taken the form of an innocent babe. He offered Otnit such splendid ransom of sword and shield to set him free, that the Emperor laid him down again, and even allowed him to hold the magic ring, by the wearing of which it had been possible for him to see what is usually hidden from mortal sight.

Now it was Elberich's turn, and being once more invisible, he teased the Emperor to his heart's content, dwelling on the anger of the Queen-Mother should she find that her gift was lost. Not until the Emperor was out of patience, and on the point of riding away did Elberich restore the ring to him.

'And now, O Otnit,' he said, 'since I see you love well your mother, whom I loved long ere you saw the light, I will help you to gain your bride.'

And Otnit was glad, for he knew that the word of a Dwarf is ever as good as his bond.

In the spring of the year, 'when all the birds were singing,' the Emperor called his friends together and bade them embark their troops with his in the ships at anchor in the harbour. The waters of the bay gleamed as a field of gold as the stately vessels glided over them, and for long the carols of the birds on shore went with them on the breeze. Otnit's hopes were high as he paced the deck, though he grieved that the Dwarf had not come to join him.

At length the fleet reached the Eastern coast of the Mediterranean, and there King Otnit beheld a haven full of ships, far more in number than his own. 'I would that Elberich were here, for he is skilled in warfare,' he murmured uneasily, for his men looked askance at the fleet before them. The words had barely left his lips when the sound of a laugh came from aloft, and straightway the Dwarf displayed himself. He had been in hiding amongst the rigging, and was now at hand to use his Fairy powers in Otnit's service.

Elberich's gift of a small round stone, which he bade him thrust into his cheek, conferred upon Otnit the gift of language, and enabled him to impersonate a rich merchant with so much success that his ship was allowed to drop anchor in the harbour. When dusk had fallen, and all was quiet, the Emperor disembarked, encamping with his troops among the rock-hewn burial places of the ancient Phœnicians, which abounded on that coast. Here he abode for three whole days, while Elberich sought the King of Syria, demanding his daughter's hand in marriage for his royal master. It was refused point blank, and, more than this, the Soldan ordered his unwelcome visitor to be put to death. But the flashing blades of the guards cut the empty air, and Elberich jeered at them finely.

Elberich had jeered him finely.

'Your daughter shall go to my lord of her own free will,' he cried to the Soldan, 'and only so shall your skull be saved!' He then returned to the Emperor, who bade his troops attack the city of Sidon.

A desperate battle with the heathen followed; for awhile the enemy's numbers triumphed, but not for long. The Emperor's charge swept all before him, and the Soldan's soldiers fell like corn before the scythe. Then the Dwarf led the army to the Syrian capital; and red as had been the field of Sidon, it was as nothing to that of Muntabur, where men's blood flowed as a crimson river.

While yet the battle was at its height, Elberich made his way, unseen, to an inner chamber of the Royal Palace, and though he had come to rate the Princess for her father's obstinacy, words forsook him in her presence. So fair a maid he had never seen; her mouth 'flamed like the rose,' her flowing hair was the colour of rich red gold, and her lovely eyes had the radiance of the moon. Elberich drew her to the window, and by the aid of his power over space, showed her King Otnit in the thick of the fight. The sun fell full on his upturned face, as, seated on his white charger, he rallied his men for the final onslaught; he looked as brave a knight as the Princess had ever seen, and she lowered her glance as Elberich told her how she could save her father.

'Death alone can wean King Otnit's desire to wed you,' he said. 'His love for you passes the love of man, and is withal as tender as that of a woman for her child.'

Much more Elberich spake to her to the same purpose, and at close of day she allowed him to lead her where he would. Together they passed through a secret passage beneath the Palace, and so through the royal gardens, to a path which wound down to the field of battle.

Fighting had ceased for awhile, for the heathen had been sore smitten; and since his men had neither eaten nor slept for many long hours, the Emperor must needs let them rest until dawn. Full of impatience at the delay which kept him from storming the walls that held the lady of his love, he paced his tent, and turned to find her standing before him. Her mouth flamed red as the reddest rose; her eyes had the lustre of the harvest moon, and her red-gold hair framed a snowy brow that was white as the breast of a swan. Bending his knee, he touched with his lips the hem of her gown, and when the Princess gave him her exquisite hand, he could scarce breathe for rapture.

"'She is yours, O Otnit!' cried the Dwarf"

'She is yours, O Otnit!' cried the Dwarf; and the Emperor lifted her on to his charger, speaking to her with such tender and kindly words that her fears were stilled. With Elberich perched on the horse's mane, they straightway rode to the coast, where the sails of the Emperor's vessel swelled roundly in the wind. On the summer seas of the blue Mediterranean, they two were wed; and never had mortal man a sweeter wife, or maid a more gallant husband."

When the Dwarf had come to the end of his story, he very politely bade me goodbye, and bowed me out of his Castle. A week or two later we went to Saltzburg, and there I had a real adventure.

The Professor with whom we were staying hadn't a single grandchild, and as all his books were old and dusty, to say nothing of being written in German, I should have found it rather dull if he had not lent me his nephew's pony. I had learnt to ride as a little chap, when we lived in the country. It was lovely there, but no one was ever ill, and Father had so few patients that we could not stay.

The pony's name was Heinrich. He knew his way everywhere, the Professor said, so Father didn't mind my riding him alone, and I had a ripping time.

One day we went to the Wunderberg, a big hill on a wide bleak moor, which was supposed to be quite hollow, and the favourite haunt of Wild Women.

The ground was extremely bumpy, and several times I was almost thrown out of the saddle. At last I got off, for I thought I would rather walk.

It was a splendid morning, and I was glad that I wasn't the Professor's nephew, away at school, as I lay on my back and looked up at the sky.

A small black beetle crawled over my hand, but I was so comfortable that I scarcely stirred. It crossed my cuff and climbed a blade of grass; and as I watched it a shadow fell between me and the sunlight.

A slender woman in a white gown was standing close to me. Her face was thin, and very wistful, and over her shoulders, down to her very feet, fell a mantle of glistening yellow hair.

"Are you hungry, child?" she asked gently, holding out to me a slice of fine white bread.

"Not yet," I answered, for we had had *Sauerkraut* for breakfast, and I felt that I should not want anything more to eat for a long time. She looked disappointed, and sighed as she threw the bread away. A bird flew down and pecked it, but after a taste or two he left it where it was.

"Then surely you are thirsty, and will drink from my horn?" she pleaded, showing me a silver vessel with curious scrolls and writings traced in gold, which had been hidden by her beautiful hair. I took a sip from its bevelled edge, and had scarcely swallowed the first drop when I felt myself sinking through the hill, the Wild Woman still beside me.

"At last! At last!" she cried, clapping her shadowy hands as we stood in a wide hall lit with amber light. "O sisters, rejoice with me! I have found a child, and his eyes, his eyes are crystal clear."

She bent over me as she spoke, half smothering me with her silken tresses, and I was so afraid that those sisters of hers would hug me too, that I scrambled away and I took to my heels and *ran*.

But you couldn't get far in that place. It was a miniature town, with silver streets and golden houses, and gorgeous palaces in between. Every turn I took led to a wide square filled with rose trees, where fountains of gold and silver water bubbled and sparkled in the mysterious pale green light. A flock of brilliant humming birds whirred their wings in my face so that I could not see where I was going, and the Wild Women formed a circle round me and began to sing:

"Only once did mortal child,
By our silver horn beguiled,
Find a way to leave us;
Though they call us strange and wild,
Thou shalt find us soft and mild.
Stay, and do not grieve us."

Their voices were very sweet, but when they had sung that verse twice over, I did not want to hear it again.

"I don't mind staying with you for an hour or two," I said, as they stopped singing, "but I shouldn't care to live here. I am a Christmas Child, and there are other Fairy Folk I want to see."

Then they looked at each other, and drew away.

"Since he is a Christmas Child," said one, "we cannot keep him. You should have known better, Sister Snow-blossom, than to bring him here!"

"How could I tell," wailed Snow-blossom. "He seemed like any other boy, and would just have fitted the green silk suit that I wove so long ago."

"Alas, alas!" the others sighed. "The longer he stays, the more it will wring our hearts to part with him. Take him back to the hill at once, dear Snow-blossom, and bid him hasten home."

But I didn't want to go just yet, for now that they did not wish to hug me, I thought they were rather nice. Their faces were like pure marble, so still and pale, and their light green eyes were very gentle. So I asked if Snow-blossom might not show me round, as the Professors did Father when he came to a strange town. Her sisters still urged her to send me away at once, before she had time to grow fond of me, but she would not listen.

"What do you want with a mortal child?" I said, when I had been all over the empty golden houses, and had seen the tiny cathedral, the model of the one at Saltzburg, set with pearls and rubies, and many other precious stones of which I did not know the name.

"Because we are lonely," she answered; "so lonely, child. Our only friends are the little people who guard our treasures in the centre of the earth, and we would fain have mortals to bear us company. Once, long ago, a goodly youth of noble birth was almost tempted to sip from our silver horn, and had he done so his home would have known him no more. Sweet Stella, the fairest Wild Woman who drew breath between the last faint pulse of the night time and the glowing dawn of day, waylaid him on the brow of the hill when he was heated in the chase, but although he craved the cooling draught she offered him, he would not drink from her hand; her exceeding beauty excited his suspicions, and he guessed that she was no mortal maid.

'Let me see what your wine is like before I taste it!' he said warily, taking the silver horn from her hands. He had no sooner grasped it, than he sprang to his horse and rode away. For many years the horn was kept amongst the treasures of the House of Oldenburg, to which he belonged, but at last, after many generations, it came back to us. No one but you and the little Karl has drunk from it since then."

We were under the rose trees in the great square, and I had found a seat in a ruby and pearl pavillion, with queer golden faces staring down on me from each corner. Snow-blossom hid her face in her hands when I asked her who was Karl, and rocked herself to and fro; then she lifted her head and looked at me, and I saw that she was crying.

"I will tell you," she said, "but first come close. For words have wings in the Wunderberg, and I would not have my sisters know I am grieving still."

I sat down beside her, and then she began, speaking very softly and slowly, with deep sighs in between. The tears on her cheeks seemed to shine like pearls, and her hair gleamed more golden than ever.

The little Karl and the wild-woman.

"There was once a poor man named Henzel who should have been well content, for his girl-wife, Gretchen, was good and sweet, and the black bread he ate when his toil was over was pleasant to his taste. His bed was warm, and his sleep was sound. What could a man want more?

But Henzel was ever full of complainings. His neighbour, Johann, had married a rich woman, and now owned a well stocked farm with many herds. Each time that he met him, Henzel sighed.

'I might have done better than he,' he grumbled, even when he heard that Johann's wife was a great scold, and did not allow her husband a moment's peace. He looked askance at his gentle Gretchen, who bore with his rough moods tenderly, since once he had been her lover. But she grieved in secret, for never a good word had he for her now, and her flaxen hair lost its shimmer of satin, and her cheeks their dainty bloom.

She was digging in the cottage garden, for Henzel would do no work at home, when a very old man toiled slowly up the hill. His clothes were dusty, and his staff was bent; he looked very weary, and his voice, as he bade her 'Goodmorrow,' was faint and low. Gretchen's heart was filled with pity; she invited him to enter her tidy kitchen, and put before him the best she had. It was not much, but her strange guest thanked her gratefully. While he rested, she went to the forest, to cut him a strong oak sapling for a staff. The old man had vanished when she returned, and in his place sat a little Dwarf, not more than twelve inches high.

'I perceive that you have a kind disposition, Gretchen, which is better than a rich dower,' he said, waving his hand for her to be seated also. 'You are already sufficiently blessed,' he went on, 'in being both virtuous and patient, but I am willing to grant you your dearest wish. Speak out, and tell me what you most desire.'

Gretchen bent her brows, and pondered deeply. If she asked the Dwarf for gold, Henzel would rejoice, but she had lived with him long enough to know that whatever he had, he would still want more. Should she ask for another husband, then, since the one she had, had ceased to love her, and threw her but scornful looks? Nay—that would be wrong, for whatever happened she was Henzel's wife.

In the old man's place sat a little Dwarf.

And the flush on her girlish face became yet deeper, for a very sweet thought had fluttered across her mind. She would ask for a little child to lie on her breast, and bear her company through the long nights and days.

When the Dwarf heard her whispered request, he smiled on her very kindly.

'You are a true woman,' he said, and disappeared as Henzel crossed the threshold.

'Who has been here?' he asked, scowling at the empty cup and platter.

'An old, old man, who was tired and hungry,' Gretchen replied, and anxious to escape his further questioning, she turned to the newly-kindled fire, and put on a saucepan of broth for him. But Henzel was very curious, for strangers came that way but seldom, and before long he had drawn the whole story from

Gretchen's lips, with the exception of the Dwarf's offer to grant her a wish.

'Did he not speak of rewarding you for your hospitality?' her husband persisted, guessing that something had been kept back from him. And Gretchen shyly told him for what she had asked.

Fierce was Henzel's anger at her neglect of this opportunity to make him rich. He stormed and raved until poor Gretchen longed to hide, and when at last his rage had spent itself, he was sullen as winter clouds. She would have minded this more had it not been for the dear new hope that filled her bosom, and early in the spring a little son was born to her.

What cared she then for Henzel's anger, so long as it did not touch her child? It was joy enough to feel the wee thing's fingers straying over her face, to see his limbs grow round and dimpled, and to hear him laugh as she sang to him baby songs. Henzel went in and out, taking little notice of either of them; his thoughts were all absorbed in schemes for growing rich, for the love of money held him in its grip.

When little Karl was six years old his mother died. Instead of sorrowing for her, Henzel was glad, for now he could marry the elderly widow in the next town who was ready to exchange her wealth for a handsome husband.

So Henzel, too, had now a well-stocked farm, but this brought him small satisfaction. For his new wife was a greater scold even than Johann's, and he dare not so much as cross the threshold without taking off his boots. As to Karl, he was sent to mind the cattle on the Kugelmill close by; the little lad was so ill-clad that his ragged tatters blew in the winter wind. He was hungry also, for his stepmother grudged him the simplest food, and but that he shared their berries with the birds, he must have starved.

When the hawthorns were white with the snows of spring, and the daisies showed their golden centres on the grassy slopes, we heard him crying for his mother. Stella flew to his side, and gathered him in her arms. Her lovely hair covered his shivering limbs, and the desolate child clung close to her as she held the silver horn to his curved red lips. His soft embrace set her woman-love on fire, and veiling him in her golden tresses, she brought him here.

He was happy with us—as happy as the days were long. We wove for him garments of silken sheen, and taught him to call us by the sweet name of 'Mother.' … One day he begged us to let him play on the hill, so we took him thither, hiding close by, that we might guard him from harm. He was seen by some wood-cutters working near, and they took word to his father; but before he could fetch him, we had spirited him away. Karl never asked to play on the hill again, and all went well with us for many years, till he sprang into a gallant youth, with his mother's eyes and a lordly will, unlike her yielding way.

And then? Ah me! His love for our beautiful Stella grew fierce and wild—the love of a mortal man for a maid. And since no Wild Woman may wed, one night he bore her away from our hill to the evening star, which is the sanctuary of lovers. Thence she sends glad dreams to motherless children, and to lonely women who pine for love."

I did not stay much longer in the Wunderberg, for somehow the scented air seemed to have grown chilly. When I said to Snow-blossom that I must leave her, she wept again, and gave me a shining strand of hair to guide me back to the moor. It turned into gossamer when I reached the daylight, and floated softly away.

Heinrich was still munching at the short grass, and stared at me very hard when I caught his bridle. I suppose he thought I had been a long while gone.

Chapter IX
The Little White Feather.

If you've ever tried to count the raindrops,

If you've ever tried to count the raindrops, you will know how I felt when for three whole days it poured in torrents. I was alone in the library, watching a hole in the wainscotting through which a mouse had just poked her head, when some one said "*Guten Morgen*" in a piping voice, and I knew this must be a Kobold. I was rather surprised that I had not met one of these House-Spirits before.

He was sitting on the edge of a bookcase—a little brown man with a wrinkled, good-natured face, and wearing no clothes. He chuckled when I said that I would rather speak English if he did not mind, and remarked that all languages were the same to him.

"I believe you have met some cousins of mine, the Brownies," he went on affably, kissing his hand to the mouse, who popped back to her hole as if he had shocked her. "They are good little chaps, but quiet and humdrum. You always know what a Brownie will do, but as for us—mortals can never tell what a Kobold will be up to next. We make ourselves quite at home in their houses, and really own them, if the truth were known. But excuse me—I should not appear before you in this undress."

In the twinkling of an eye the Kobold had changed himself into a curly haired boy, with smooth pink cheeks and a red silk coat, and knickerbockers of dark green velvet. "This is my best suit," he explained proudly, turning himself from side to side. "I usually wear it when I play with children who were born, like yourself, at the blessed feast of Christmas-tide. It is only one of my many disguises, however, though I seldom allow myself to be seen at all. I can even hide in the cast-off coat of a harmless snake, and woe to him who lays stick upon me or seeks to drive me away. The Heinzelmänchen, as we are called, can be bitter foes as well as powerful friends, and 'twas an evil day for the city of Köln when we marched out of it. It has never prospered since."

"Why——" I began, and the Kobold held up his hand to stop me, puckering his baby face into a dreadful frown.

"Why? Why? Why?" he mimicked. "How like the child of mortal man! Everything has to tell its reason—you rob the peach of its velvet bloom that you may find the secret of its ruddy splendour, and the fairy gems on the grass at dawn are to you but water distilled from earth! You would know how the tide finds a way to turn, why the light of the stars transcends your rush-lights! Elves and Fairies and such-like things are driven away by your curiosity, as the Heinzelmänchen were by Rosetta."

I was going to ask who Rosetta might be, but I remembered just in time that this would be another question. The Kobold chose a more comfortable seat, and told me of his own accord.

The Sin of Rosetta.

"Toward the end of the eighteenth century," he began, "the Heinzelmänchen, took up their abode in the city of Köln, where Johann Farina distilled the sweet-scented waters now famous all over the world. When first he blended the fragrant oils of bergamot, citron, orange and rosemary, it was we who whispered to him in what proportion he should mix them, and how to imprison their lasting perfume. Not only him did we help, but wherever we came across a worthy fellow who was poor but honest, we gave him a lift up; such was Rudolph the tailor, whom we found when a lad on the steps of the great Cathedral, without a *pfennig* in his pocket, and with a wolf inside him big enough to swallow a little pig. When we saw how readily he returned a *thaler* that rolled to his feet to the feeble old woman who had dropped it, though he might well have said he had not seen it fall, we took him to our hearts, and swore to befriend him.

'So!' we said, one to the other. 'Rudolph is worthy to be our comrade. He is a good lad, and henceforth we will see that he does not want.'

The first thing to be done was to procure him decent clothing, for no one would employ him while he went in rags. We did this by pointing him out to the wife of a rich merchant, who fancied she saw in his pinched white face a likeness to the son she had lost long since.

Touched by the poor lad's poverty, she gave him a suit of clothes which had lain by for many a day, and on finding he was an orphan, apprenticed him to a tailor. The lad worked well. We took it in turns to sit beside him, showing him just where to place his needle, so that his seams were always neat, and guiding his scissors so that he cut the cloth to the best advantage. So skilful did he become that, when his time was out, his master begged him to stay on with him as head assistant, and gave him a good wage.

A fine young spright was Rudolph now, with jet-black hair and eyes like coals. His master's daughters, Euralie and Rosetta, both looked on him with favour, and for a time it seemed that he knew not which to choose. Euralie was small and slight, with eyes like a dove's; Rosetta was tall and buxom, and had she been free from the vice of curiosity would have made him a model wife. She was clever and industrious as well as witty, and when Dark Rudolph passed by the gentle Euralie, and took Rosetta for his betrothed, it was only the Heinzelmänchen who shook their heads.

Never was grander wedding feast than his. While he and Rosetta where still in church, we brought to his house the finest drinking vessels that we could lay our hands on, and pots and pans of beaten copper that were the envy of every housewife bidden as a guest. There were fairy cakes in the silver dishes, and luscious fruits such as grew in no western lands; the wine in the ruby goblets was honeyed nectar, and though his friends quaffed deeply, their heads remained quite clear. A proud man was

Rudolph as he drank to his bride, and she looked so happy and gay and bright, that we resolved to take her, too, under our protection.

And this we did. When her children came, we rocked the cradle and sang them lullabies while she baked and brewed, and when they slept we scrubbed and polished from garret to cellar, until her house was the pride of the street. Often she would ask to be allowed to see us, but we always refused, telling her to respect our wish, and be content. Still she would not rest, and nothing that Dark Rudolph could say to her would induce her to hold her peace.

He had now three shops instead of one, and counted lords and barons among his customers. No one could fit as he could, for we were always at hand to nip in here or let out there, and many a fine straight figure was the result of our cunning skill. His fame spread far through the neighbouring towns, and one spring a great noble travelled to Köln to order some rich apparel for himself and his suite. Our busy tailor was at his wit's end how to get it finished in time, for all his assistants were working their hardest, and still they were behind.

'Have no fear! Dark Rudolph,' we cried, when we found him alone. 'Send your men to rest, and leave it to us. When you wake in the morning you shall find all done.'

We lost not a moment that livelong night—it was as if our needles had wings. Just before cockcrow, the door of the workroom creaked softly open, and there stood Rosetta in her white nightgown, with her hair in two long plaits, peering round the corner to see if she could catch us at work. We were justly enraged, but since we heard her in time to render ourselves invisible, and also because we loved Dark Rudolph, we decided to give her one more chance.

It was our custom to leave the lower part of the house at the hour of midnight, no matter what we might be doing, and climb the steep stairs that led to the bedrooms, to watch that the ghosts which were free to roam till cockcrow might not ruffle the children's hair, or wake them with their long-drawn sighs. Rosetta knew this, for she had often heard us comforting the little Rudolph when his sleep was disturbed by a bad dream, and with gross ingratitude she tried to be-fool us. One night, she strewed dried peas on the top steps of the winding staircase, so that when we came up we should lose our footing and fall to the bottom, and thus she might see us struggling on the ground. We knew perfectly well, however, why she had bought the peas, and stayed below. When she rose next morning, she forgot the trap she had laid for us, and tumbled headlong down the stairs. While she groaned and moaned over her broken ankle, the Heinzelmänchen marched out of the town to stirring music, which was heard by all the citizens. We sailed down the Rhine in a phantom boat, which you may yet see floating on its waters if you look for it at the right time. And Dark Rudolph and his Rosetta sighed for our help in vain."

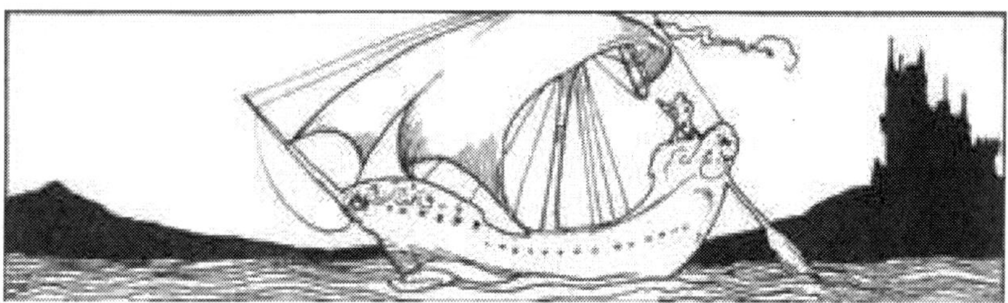

The Kobold was a most entertaining little fellow, and stayed with me all the morning, telling me of well known House Spirits of days gone by. One of these tales was about

The Little white Feather.

"Hinzelmann," said the Kobold solemnly, "was a Spirit who haunted the castle of Hudemühlen, though it was not until late in the sixteenth century that those who lived there were aware of his presence. He seemed of so friendly a disposition that the servants became quite used to him. They never saw him, but he would often talk with them while they worked, telling them of what went on in the Underworld, and of the mighty Giants of bye-gone days who had been created in order to protect the Dwarfs from savage beasts, but had become themselves so savage in the course of the ages that they had to be done away with. In time the lord of the castle heard of his strange visitor, and sent him a message saying he desired his presence at a certain hour.

'No need to wait until then, good Sir!' laughed Hinzelmann over his shoulder. 'I assist each morning at your lordship's toilet, though you do not perceive me, and I blunt your razors when you are out of temper.'

This displeased the lord of the castle, for he thought it unseemly to be on terms of such familiar intimacy with a bodiless House-Spirit. When he rebuked him for his presumption, Hinzelmann laughed more loudly still. 'Better men than you have to put up with my company, if I will!' he cried, 'and, believe me, I do not intend to leave you!'

The nobleman grew more and more uneasy, for it disturbed him to feel that he was never alone. Hinzelmann whistled and sang through the State rooms, and when his lordship expressed irritation this was the House-Spirit's favourite song:

'If thou here wilt let me stay,
Good luck shalt thou have alway.
But if hence thou dost me chase,
Luck will ne'er come near the place.'

[1]

He hummed this morning, noon, and night, until the lord of the castle was sick of it. 'Since I cannot drive this fellow away,' he said at last, 'I must e'en go myself;' and telling no one of his intentions, he summoned his coach and set out for Hanover. On the way he noticed that no matter how fast his horses went, a little white feather danced above their heads. Although he wondered at this, he did not connect it with the House-Spirit, and when he arrived at his chosen Inn, sought his couch with a mind at ease.

'Thank heaven,' he muttered, as he turned him over and went to sleep, 'I am free at last of this troublesome Hinzelmann. By the time I see fit to return home, he may have gone elsewhere.'

Next morning he missed his fine gold chain, which was an heirloom, and, greatly distressed, he haughtily demanded of the Innkeeper that his servants should be searched.

'They have robbed me,' he cried, 'and they shall suffer for it! Cannot one sleep at your house without meeting with knaves and thieves?'

A little white Feather danced above their heads.

At this the Innkeeper was very angry. Instead of condoling with the nobleman on his loss, and offering to make it good, he roundly rebuked him for taking away the character of honest men without due proof. The noble was leaving the Inn in much haste when a soft voice asked him why he was troubled.

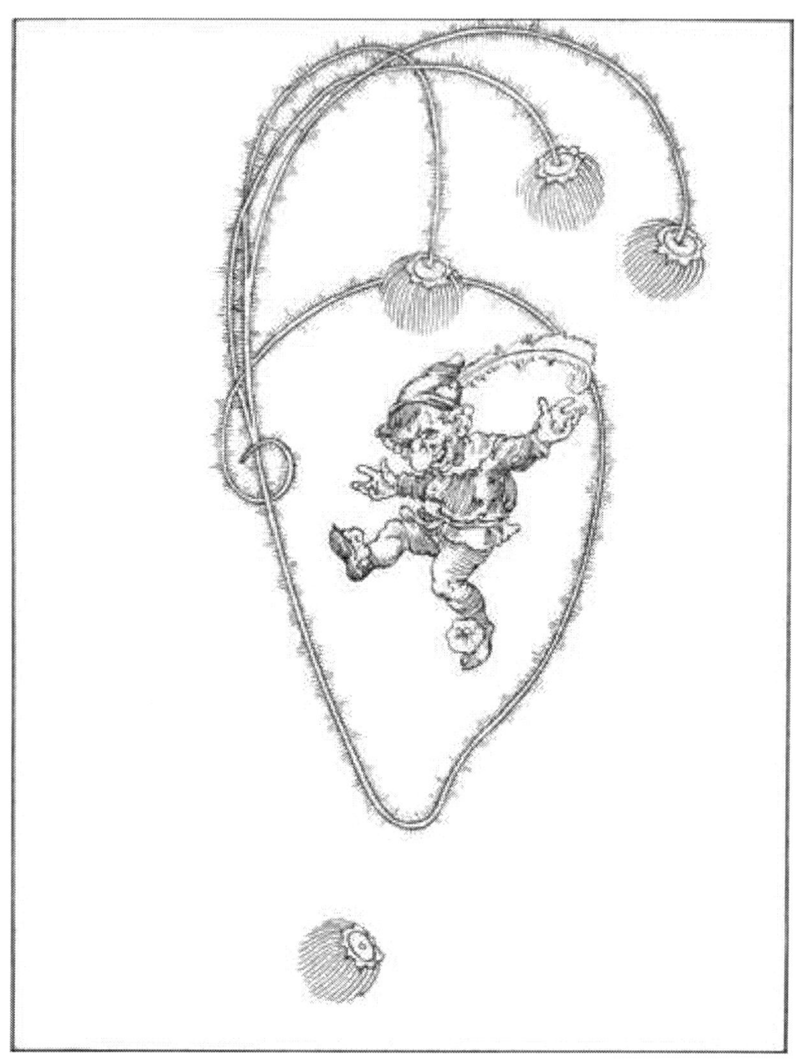

'If it be on account of the bauble upon which you set such store,' it continued, 'look under your pillow and you will find it. You cannot get on without Hinzelmann after all!'

'I would I had never known you, base spirit!' stormed the nobleman. 'You have put me greatly in the wrong with all these men, and my journey has been for nought, since you are here. If you do not quit me I will leave this country; it is not wide enough to hold us both.'

Then Hinzelmann spoke to him with much reason, pointing out that he wished him no harm, and that it was impossible to shake him off, since wherever the lord went, he could follow.

'It was I who flew as a little white feather in front of your coach,' he concluded. 'You played the part of a poltroon when you fled from what you believed to be evil, instead of fighting it on your own ground. Come back with me, and if you give me your friendship, I will work but good to you and yours.'

So the nobleman went back to his castle, and Hinzelmann lived there with him. A little room was set aside for his use in an upper story, and here they placed, by the nobleman's orders, a small round table, and a tiny bed. No one could ever make out if he slept on this, but once when the cook entered very quickly, to take him the dish of new milk and wheaten crumbs which was placed each morn on his table, she saw a shallow depression on the down pillow, as if something very small and soft had rested there.

When the time came for Hinzelmann to leave the castle, he presented its lord with three fairy gifts, the last of these being a leather glove richly wrought with pearls in a curious pattern of snails and scrolls. So long as this glove was in possession of his house, he told him, so long would his race flourish. And thus he requited the kindness which had been shown him. There is nothing that we like better than to help our friends."

"I know," I said, nodding my head. And the House Spirit smiled as if this pleased him.

"We need take no credit for this," he remarked, "since the Dwarf King himself sets us the example. His rescue of the poor old couple at Schillingsdorf is but one of many instances of the way in which he gladly helps those who show hospitality to him or his.

Caught in a storm, he wandered from door to door, entreating each person who answered his knock to let him enter and warm himself. One and all they refused, for his green velvet garments were stained and draggled, and they had not the wit to see that in spite of his dripping clothes and dishevelled beard he was still every whit a king. At last he came to the hut of an ancient shepherd, whose little old wife was as thin as he, for food had been very scarce. The moment she saw the wanderer, her heart went out to him.

'Come in and welcome, you poor little fellow!' she said, setting wide her door. 'Our fire is not much to boast of, but 'tis better than none on a night like this.' And the shepherd hobbled to the inner room that he might bring his Sunday coat, and place this round their visitor's shoulders while his own lay drying on the hearth. Then the old woman spread a white cloth on the table, and gave the Dwarf her share of the coarse black bread which was all her cupboard contained.

'I thank you, my friends,' he said, breaking the bread into two fragments. As he did so, one became a fine white loaf, and the other a noble cheese. The Dwarf laughed at the old couple's amazement, and bade them feast to their heart's content.

'So long as you leave on the platter a crust of bread and an inch of cheese,' he said, 'so long will a fresh loaf and a fresh cheese spring from these fragments during the night; but if ever a beggar entreats your help, and you refuse him, they will turn to dust and ashes. Now I bid you farewell, but ere long we shall meet again.'

So saying, he went out in the rain, despite their entreaties that he would at least stay with them until the storm was over.

Little sleep did they have that night, for wind and rain swept through the valley. Torrents roared down the mountain side, flooding the wooden houses, and even worse befell at daybreak. An enormous rock snapped off from a topmost peak, and carrying with it great masses of stones and uprooted firs, crashed down on the little village. All living things were buried beneath its weight except the shepherd and his wife, whose cottage yet was spared. Tremblingly they stood on the threshold, for they thought their last hour had come.

'Thou hast been a good wife, my dear one,' breathed the shepherd, as he drew her frail form close to him.

'It is well that we should go together, since thou hast lain by my side for nigh sixty years,' she whispered, hiding her face against his breast.

'How now?' cried a reassuring voice. 'Dost despair so easily?' And looking up they saw their friend the Dwarf riding on a rough raft in the centre of the stream, and steering before him the trunk of an immense pine. This he proceeded to fix crosswise in front of their little garden, so as to form a dam. The torrent now passed by the cottage, leaving it undisturbed, and the voice of the wind was hushed. The sun came out, and the birds sang; but the only people alive in Schillingsdorf were the shepherd and his old wife."

"'How now?' cried a reassuring voice."

The forest paths were dappled with sunlight as Father and I strolled down its winding glades, and all the wood things were chirping and chattering with joy. Now and then something brown and furry scuttled across our path, and once I all but trod on a tiny mouse, who had hidden herself under last year's leaves.

"You clumsy boy!" said a tiny voice, and I turned in time to catch sight of a wee pink Elf as she sprang from the flower Father wore in his button hole upon a bright blue butterfly which had been hovering above her for some time, and now darted swiftly away.

After a while we came to an open space where the woodmen had been felling timber. Several great trees still lay on the ground; one was particularly straight and round, and I noticed three wide crosses cut deep into the bark. I thought I would like to carve my name there too, for my knife had been most beautifully sharp since the *Nain Rouge* touched it, so when Father sat down soon afterward to read his letters, I went straight back to the spot. As I reached it I heard the distant baying of hounds; the sound came nearer and nearer, and mingling with it were shouts in a strange deep voice, which almost frightened me. As I looked up, my knife was jerked out of my hand by a little woman dressed in green, who pushed me breathlessly aside and sat down, sobbing bitterly, on the middle cross. I was still staring at her when there flashed through the air a huntsman on a fiery horse, followed by many hounds. Their hurrying feet knocked off my cap and rumpled all my hair. They had passed in a second, and next moment I heard their baying far away.

The little woman in green sobbed still, but she seemed to be growing calmer. Her hair and eyes were a soft light grey, and her frock was most prettily trimmed with tufts of moss.

"Aha!" I thought when I noticed this, "you are one of the Moss-women, I've no doubt." For I knew that these were supposed to haunt the forests of Southern Germany.

"That was the Wild Huntsman," said the little thing, looking at me trustfully. "But for the kindness of the woodcutters who make these marks in the trees they fell, I should have fallen to his bow and spear. When we can find three crosses we are safe, for he dare not touch us then."

I waited to hear what else she would say, for I thought of the Kobold's "*Why? Why? Why?*" and did not like to ask her questions. In a little while her lips were smiling, and swaying to and fro, as a tree sways in the wind, she began to sing. I knew I had heard that song before, but I could not think where until I remembered that the pines which rustled against the windows of my night nursery had often sung it when I was small.

"It's the song of the wind," she told me, "and the very first sound we hear. We are born in the roots of the tree which is to be our home, and when this dies, we must die too. So long as the sap runs through its branches, and the bark is not cut or injured, we are safe and sound in our snug recess, but at certain times we are bound to leave it, to seek for food, or to attend our lords. It is then that we are in such grave danger—and all because Elfrida tried her witcheries on a stranger."

"What did she do?" I could not help asking.

"I will tell you," said the Moss-woman sadly, "and then you will understand why even the youngest of us has now grey hair."

The Wild Huntsman.

"Elfrida was the fairest of our race," she sighed, "and her palace the tallest and straightest pine that ever raised its boughs to Heaven. When she left its shelter at early dawn to bathe in some sparkling stream, or seek for sweet berries in the thickets, the Flower-Elves flocked to greet her; wild roses gave her their bloom for her oval cheeks, and the violets scented her sunny hair. Wherever she passed, the moss grew a brighter green, and she had but to breathe on a gnarled old trunk, and the softest feathery fronds came to hide its ugliness. The creatures of the forest were all her friends, and took pride, as we did, in her loveliness.

'Have a care, Elfrida—a stranger comes!' cried a squirrel one summer morning, staying his dancing feet to warn her. His up-cocked ears had caught the thud of some well-shod charger's swift approach, and he guessed he would not be riderless.

'Go back to thy palace, dear child!' cooed a motherly pigeon who had reared many broods of snowy fledglings, and misdoubted the sparkle in Elfrida's pale green eyes.

'Haste thee home, Elfrida!' cried the stream as it gurgled over the stones; 'haste thee home, and hide thy face from the sunlight.' But Elfrida pretended not to hear as she shook out the crystal drops from her gorgeous hair.

The horse and his rider were close to her now; the huntsman blew his golden horn, and in the excitement of the chase might have passed her by, unseeing, but for his hounds. In a moment they had surrounded her, baying like hungry wolves, and Elfrida sprang to a branch that overhung the water, where her white limbs gleamed against its green. The huntsman sent the dogs to heel, and dismounting from his horse, entreated the maiden to come down to him. Nothing loth, Elfrida coyly descended, and the huntsman was amazed anew at her perfect form. He sat at her feet through the hush of noonday, and at even he was there still. When the moon turned the glades to silver, Elfrida left him, but she promised to meet him again next day, and he could not sleep for thinking of her.

But although she smiled on him sweetly as she lay on the banks of the stream, and listened with languid pleasure to his fond fierce wooing, which passed for her many an idle hour, she would not consent to be his wife.

'I like best the gems that I find on the lilies at daybreak,' she said, when he vowed that the richest jewels that the earth could give should deck her fair white arms. 'You must offer me something rarer than these if I am to forsake my kindred to go with you.'

Then the huntsman swore that he would give her all he had; only his honour would he hold back, for he was sick with love and longing.

Now behind Elfrida's loveliness dwelt a spirit of malice and wanton cruelty, and though she loved not this wild Huntsman, and had no intention of being his bride, she wished to see how far her power over him could go. So she asked of him these three things: the crest of his House cut in the stone over his castle gates, where it had stood for centuries; the leaf from his dead mother's Bible, whereon she had written the date of her marriage day, with the names of the children born to her; and his father's sword.

'Nay, Sweetheart!' cried the Huntsman. 'Ask me for aught else in the world, but not for these things, since they touch my honour!'

'These will I have, and nothing less,' said Elfrida wilfully, looking at him through her long gold lashes until his soul went out from him. His face was white as milk as he rode away, and the creatures of the forest cringed with shame. For they knew she had asked what was unseemly; and they ceased to attend her when she went to the stream at dawn.

He entreated the Maiden to come down.

When the moon was at her full the Huntsman returned with the three gifts, and now he thought to take Elfrida in his arms. But she thrust him from her with bitter words, tearing the leaf from the sacred Book into a thousand shreds, and tossing the crest and sword into the running stream.

'What!' she cried, and her scornful laugh rang through the woodland, 'shall I, Elfrida, be the sport of a man who holds the honour of his house as something less than a maiden's whim?

I will have none of you—get you gone!' And she flung out her arms to the strong North Wind, who caught her to him and bore her off. But not to her high pine palace did he take her, for he was angry because of her cruelty; and far away at the grim North Pole, she shivers yet under the thickest ice. Her green eyes shine through the frost-bound floes, and light the depths of the Northern seas."

"And the Huntsman?" I questioned.

"He died in his rage, where Elfrida left him!" said the Moss-woman mournfully, "and his spirit seeks still to avenge his wrongs. To the last of our race it will pursue us, until none of our kindred lives."

"Chris! Chris! where are you?"

It was Father's voice, and the Moss-woman vanished. Father wanted to read me a funny letter from the Locust, who complained a lot of being called up at night by patients who had no money, and wouldn't have paid him even if they had. This was the way they often treated Father, but he said "Poor beggars!" and then forgot it, while the Locust was very cross.

Next day I went back to the forest, hoping to find the Moss-woman again, but she was not there. I found instead an Elf who was almost too small to be seen. She told me that she and her sisters lived in the cells which make leaves so green, and mixed things they drew in from the air and sunlight with the water that came through the roots, turning these into sugar to feed the tree. It sounded like magic, and I was so much interested that I almost forgot to ask about the Moss-women.

"Poor little things!" said the Leaf-Elf kindly, when I said I had seen one. "It is well that the woodcutters are their friends, or they would fare badly. Many a meal did they have from them in past times, and even Hans the Unlucky never grudged them what he gave. They paid him back for it, never fear, for they do not forget a kindness."

"Who was he?" I asked. And this is what she told me.

"Of all the unlucky mortals, Hans was surely the most to be pitied, for though he was honest and frugal, nothing he touched seemed to prosper. The farm had done well in his father's lifetime, but after he died there was not one good season for three bad ones. Far from being idle, Hans was up before dawn, and still hard at work at sundown.

The Luck of Hans.

His mother sent away her maids, since she could not pay them their wages, and kept the house straight herself; where could you find a worthier pair? But Hans' affairs went from bad to worse, and when (at the busiest time of the year) his mother lost her sight and became quite blind it was clear he was born to be unlucky.

The farm went to rack and ruin, and there came a time when Hans was forced to go off to the forest to fell a tree that his poor old mother might have fuel to warm her. When the sun was high, he drew out his lunch, and a poor little Moss-woman stole out from the undergrowth to beg a few crumbs for her hungry children.

'Take it all!' he cried, thrusting his bread into her tiny hands. 'It is waste of good food for a man to eat who is as unlucky as I.'

'I cannot repay you in kind, friend Hans,' said the Moss-woman, 'but I will give you some good advice. In the house by the mill lives a sweet young girl, with a face tinged with pink like a daisy's. She has loved you long, for you are her mate. Take her to wife, and your luck will turn.'

Hans flushed deep crimson beneath his tan, and the veins on his forehead grew tense and hard.

'You—you—' he stammered; 'you must mean Elsa? And Elsa, you say, Elsa cares for *me?* It can't—it can't—be true.'

'A woman's heart goes where it will,' answered the Moss-woman. 'Try your luck, friend Hans, and lose no time. Life is short, and the days are flying.'

Hans went at once to the house by the mill, for had he not gazed at it time and again as the casket which held his treasure?

When Elsa saw him coming with that look upon his face, she twisted a ribbon, blue as her eyes, in the pale gold plait that crowned her head, and went shyly down to meet him.

Hans said not a word, but he found a way to make her understand, and his eyes spoke, though his lips were dumb.

They were betrothed and married within the month, and little cared sweet Elsa that her friends marvelled at her choice. She comforted the sad blind dame, whose son was now her husband, as a happy woman comforts one who fears she has lost all, and behold! the old woman smiled again. As to Hans, the neighbours scarcely recognised him when they met him in the markets; she trimmed his beard, did Elsa, with her own hands, and mothered him as if he were a child of seven. His fields grew green, and then golden with harvest; his scanty flocks increased and multiplied.

'Hans' luck has changed!' the neighbours said, and they scoffed at him no more.

"Went shyly down to meet him"

But good luck itself does not last for ever, and after three years of plenty came a bad one for all in those parts. There was a long and unusual drought, followed by so much rain that the roots rotted in the ground, and sickness spread amongst sheep and oxen. Hans lost all that he had re-gained, and to add to his misfortunes, he chopped his hand instead of a log of wood, and could do no work for weeks. He was in despair, and the old blind woman beside his hearth wept and wailed from morn till eve.

'I would I were dead,' she moaned. 'I am a useless burden, for I cannot even knit. My store of wool is exhausted, and we have no money to buy more.'

'Dear Mother,' said Elsa tenderly, 'who has a greater right than you to the last penny that Hans possesses? You carried him on your breast when he was small and helpless, and have loved him faithfully all these years!'

But the mother turned her face to the wall and wrung her idle hands.

Then Elsa sold the ring that had been her lover's gift in order to buy for her soft white bread and warming cordials, and wool wherewith to ply her needles. As she returned home with her basket, grieving to think of the pain of those she loved, a Moss-woman accosted her in the forest.

'I have nought for my children to eat,' she said. And Elsa, pitying her the more that she herself was hungry, gave her a share of what she had, even to a skein of the wool, that she might weave a coat for her crying babe.

'Wait for me here!' cried the Moss-woman earnestly, and Elsa leaned sadly against a tree, too weary to be surprised. In a moment or two the Moss-woman returned, carrying a grey ball of wool and some chips of wood.

'Give the wool to the old crone who weeps by your hearth,' said the little thing, 'and the chips to Hans. He is lucky in his wife, if in nought else!'

So saying, she disappeared, and Elsa went quickly home. Thinking to win a laugh from her husband, she opened her apron to show him the Moss-woman's gifts, and, to her amazement, found that the chips had turned to yellow gold, and the little grey ball of wool into a large one of fleecy whiteness, so soft and thick that it felt like velvet! The golden chips stocked the farm again, for they were of pure metal, and weighty, and the ball of white wool was never exhausted during the old woman's life time.

She knitted away until her hundredth year, and when, long afterward, the summons came also for Hans and Elsa, in their turn, their children had good cause to bless the name of the Moss-woman."

It was to Italy we travelled next, to stay with the Signor, who had lived in England once, and was a patient of Father's.

It was fearfully hot when we arrived, and most English people had gone away; but Father and I could bear a lot of sunshine, and we did not go out in the middle of the day.

In the early mornings I went off to explore while Father was still asleep. Sometimes I made for the hills, but often I chose the city, for I liked to wander through the streets and make friends with the chattering children. They were jolly little beggars, with bare brown feet and thick dark hair that fell over their faces. My favourites were Giovanni and Mariannina; their mother worked for a grand Contessa who lived not far from the Signor. Giovanni was thin as a reed, but Mariannina, whose curly head did not reach her brother's shoulders, was as plump as a partridge, and her cheeks were red instead of brown. Adelina, the Signor's housekeeper, told me their names, and that Mariannina was the pride and torment of Giovanni's life.

"He adores her," she said, "but she is surely bewitched. She runs from him like a squirrel, and is an imp for mischief. Ah, the poor Giovanni—he has his hands full!"

After this I often met them, and if Mariannina were in a good humour she would smile at me through her lashes, while if she were cross she would frown like a Witch, and even shake her tiny fist. At this, Giovanni would look quite shocked, and would beg me in broken English not to be hurt at '*la sorellina's*' unkindness.

"She so ver' small!" he pleaded wistfully, and this was always his excuse for her.

One day she took it into her head to run away from him, and darted into the middle of the road, almost under the heels of some prancing horses. I happened to be close by, and seized her red skirt just in time to drag her back. Panting with terror, Giovanni took her from me, and when he found she was not hurt, for the first time in his life he shook her. And then he tried to kiss my hands; I almost wished I had left Mariannina to be run over. Before I could get away from him, he had thrust upon me the small gilt cage he always carried about with him, and had but just now tossed on the ground. It held his cherished '*grillo*,' or cricket, a curious pet of which all his playmates seemed very fond.

"It is yours, it is yours!" he cried, and seemed so grieved when I tried to give it back to him that I was obliged to keep it.

The cricket was a merry little creature, with a very loud voice for his size. "*Cree-cree-cree!*" he chirped, as I carried him to the villa, and he never once stopped all day. I believe that he sang the whole night through, for I heard him in my dreams; and when I woke I determined to set him free.

I carried the little gilt cage up the slope of a hill before I opened the door. No sooner had he hopped on the grass, when his "*Cree-cree-cree*" was taken up by hundreds of other crickets, who gathered round him in great excitement, chirping with all their might. As I put my fingers into my ears, a little old woman appeared from nowhere, and with a wave of her hand sent them all away.

"Many mouths make a small noise great," she said, "and you are not the first to be wearied by the crickets' song. The Sorcerer of the Seven Heads[2] liked it as little as you did, and the White Princess owes her happiness to this. I say what I know, for I am her Fairy Godmother."

"Why, they told me there were no Fairies in Italy!" I cried. And then I was sorry that I had spoken, for the little old woman grew pale with rage.

"No Fairies?" she exclaimed. "Ah, foolish ones, worse than blind! Had you not believed them you had seen countless Witches and Fays ere this, for Ascension Day has come and gone, and they are all set free. Besides these, there are Goblins and Spirits, and fearsome Incubas, and shadowy Fates who sway men's destinies. All these abound in our sunny Italy for those who have eyes to see; and there are also Fairy Godmothers, such as I. The maidens for whom I stand sponsor comb jewels out of their hair;

diamonds and pearls, rubies, and shining turquoise. But the White Princess' were always pearls; and pearls often turn to tears."

Then, drawing close to me, as I sat in the long grass, she told me of

The White Princess.

"The fates had dowered Queen Catherine with gifts; but though her husband was devoted to her, and the kingdom was blessed by a long spell of peace, she sighed unceasingly. One boon alone had been denied her, and without this she did not care to live.

'Let her have her way!' cried the Fates at last, weary of her complainings. So one summer dawn a babe was found in the bed of lilies beneath her window, and now her mourning was turned into joy. For a daughter had been her heart's desire.

The little Princess was christened Fiorita, but from the day of her birth she was known as the White Princess. Her skin was as purely pale as the petals of her guardian flowers, and the yellow gold of their stamens was the colour of her hair. But out of her eyes looked a spirit that boded sorrow—the spirit that would fain know all.

The White Princess grew lovelier day by day, smiling but seldom, and staring for hours at the distant line of the far horizon, where the hills kept watch for ever over the land Beyond. The Queen looked on with delight at the unfolding of this tender blossom, but her happiness did not bring strength, and when in due time the sweet coral lips lisped the soft word 'Mother,' her soul broke the bonds which held it, and sped away.

Fiorita was now twice orphaned, for her father, the King, would scarcely look at her, since he connected her coming with the death of his beloved wife. In order that the sight of her might not continually remind him of his sorrow, he built a fine tower of gold and crystal, and here, surrounded by all her ladies, the White Princess grew into womanhood. Lovely as snow crystals, and cold as the arctic wastes, Fiorita made few friends, and spoke to none of her inmost thoughts. The Kings of the Earth who came to woo her were abashed by her strange white beauty, and only the Prince Fiola remained to ask her hand.

He was brave as a lion, and gentle as a woman, as true knights are to this very day. The sound of his voice as he spake of his love stirred the Princess' heart to a secret joy; but him, too, she sent away with but a glance from her blue-grey eyes. And though I, her Fairy Godmother, scolded her well and entreated her to say him yea, she would not be persuaded.

'First I must see what lies hid in the land Beyond,' she said, and that very night, when the Crystal Tower shone wanly in the moon-light, and all her ladies were sleeping, the Princess covered her snow-white robe with a gossamer cloak of clouded grey, and lowered herself from her window by means of a rope of pearls, passing through her gardens and into the forest, which lay between her and the land Beyond. All fearless in her virgin purity, she listened neither to the Goblins who eyed her hungrily from the shapeless trees and besought her to show them favour, nor to the warnings of compassionate Fays who bade her return to the Crystal Tower.

"Lowered herself from her window by means of a rope of pearls"

'I seek the land Beyond,' she cried, not knowing that she could never reach it except on spirit wings.

Now the Prince Fiola could not sleep for love of her, and this night he stayed his restless wanderings in the Palace grounds by the waters of a placid lake, for the fancy came to him that therein dwelt some kindly Sprite who, perchance, would give him counsel and further his suit. Clear shone the moon above, making the smooth surface into a fairy mirror which reflected the swaying trees and the mysteries of forest depths; and as he looked, the Prince descried the shape of a slim white form which seemed to be hurrying onward amidst a forest. The poise of the head was Fiorita's; hers, too, was the queenly gait. But thinking her to be safely sleeping, the Prince believed that his eyes were cheating him, and moodily resumed his walk. When morning came, however, he hastened to the Crystal Tower. He found it in great commotion. Doors were opened and shut in rapid succession, and scared attendants ran in and out like ants.

'The Princess is not in her chamber!' her ladies told him, wringing their hands. 'Her bed has not been slept on, and her silken wrapper is still in its broidered case.'

As the Prince stood bewildered, the King came up. The remembrance of his lack of love was heavy upon him, and he strove to stifle his remorse by loud threatenings of dire punishment to all if his daughter were not speedily recovered.

As he stood quietly aside in the midst of the commotion, Prince Fiola remembered the vision of the lake, and bidding a groom go fetch him a horse, he mounted and rode straightway to the forest. Two paths stretched out before him; his horse would have taken that on the right, but the Prince urged it along the other, for he thought that he caught a glimpse of his love's white gown at the end of a woodland glade.

It was only the feather of a dove, however, and he pressed on, barely slackening his pace for hours. Darkness fell, but there was still no sign of Fiorita, and when he reached the borders of the forest, and yet had found no trace of her, his heart was sick at the thought of her peril. He could not stop, so with only the stars to guide him, he essayed to cross the waste that lay beyond, and at dawn was still riding wearily on. By the following noon both horse and rider were exhausted. The burning sun blazed down on their heads, smiting them as a sword, and though the Prince had no pity on himself, he grieved that his horse should suffer. Dismounting, he led it on until he came to a great rock, down the side of which flowed a stream of water. When he and his dumb companion had quenched their thirst, he took off its bridle and set it free, for he knew that the faithful creature could carry him no further.

'Make your way home, good friend,' he said, as he patted its glossy mane. 'I cannot return without my Princess, though I fear me 'twill be many a day before I find her.'

And now began the most toilsome part of his journey. With the land Beyond always before him, he trudged on and on, turning aside for nothing; and so passed another day and night. Now the long road wound uphill; stones blocked his way, and thorns tore his hands and face; still he pressed on, for his love was stronger than hunger and thirst, and pain had no terrors for him. Nevertheless, he had lost all hope, when a turn in the path disclosed a sight which made him for the moment forget his trouble.

A bent old woman, crooked and frail, staggered beneath a load of sticks, and dancing along at either side of her, were two rough boys, who mocked at her lameness, calling her a Witch. The Prince overtook them with rapid strides, and knowing that the power of gentleness is more lasting than that of anger, he suppressed his wrath as he spoke to them, though withal he reproved them sternly.

'Know you not,' he said, 'that only cowards persecute those who are weaker than themselves? 'Tis a woman whom you call 'mother,' and if only for this, you should hold all women in reverence. Now go—and remember what I have said. Here is something to purchase a gift for your parents. See that you are more worthy of their care.' And with other words to the same effect, he gave each a silver coin.

Won alike by his kindness and the justice of his rebuke, the boys asked pardon for their rudeness, and scampered off with glowing faces, while the old woman blessed the Prince for thus befriending her. Disclaiming her thanks, he lifted her load to his own shoulders, when it immediately became as light as air. The next moment it fell from him altogether; and he turned in great astonishment to meet her serious gaze.

'*Bel giavone!*' she exclaimed, 'I pray you think me not intrusive, but I know by your voice that your heart is heavy as the load I carried awhile ago. Tell me your grief, that if the Fates so will, I may in my turn help you.'

'In truth, good mother,' said the Prince, 'no mortal can aid me now except by telling me where I may find the White Princess, whom I seek day and night in anguish, since she is my dear love.'

'Even that can I do!' cried the old woman, straightening her bent figure until she stood before him tall and queenly, her squalid rags changing into flowing robes of purple velvet. 'I am the Witch Lucretia, and my spells are a match for those of the Sorcerer with the Seven Heads. You have travelled far from your White Princess, for the Sorcerer lurks in the forest through which you passed, and Fiorita is his prisoner. No man yet has entered his castle to leave it alive, but I will show you how this may be done, if you are willing to change your shape and become one of Earth's humblest creatures.'

The Prince feared nothing so that he might once reach the side of Fiorita, and gladly submitted himself to the enchantments of the Witch. Lucretia lifted the silver wand that was hid in the fold of her gown, and at its touch the Prince became a cricket, just such another as the one which you lately restored to liberty.

'You will find no difficulty now,' she said, 'in entering the Sorcerer's castle, for the pitfalls he has prepared for man are as nought to they who traverse the air. And that you may be one of many, and so a match for his spells, I will summon my Witches and Fairies to protect you.'

Having muttered an incantation, she blew thrice on an opalescent shell which dangled from her waist upon a ruby chain; and troops of Fays and Witches came hurrying down the road. Some were slender and stately, with faces as fair as dreamland; some were twisted and bent, and some so small that a dozen could hide in the cup of a flower. With a second wave of her silver wand, Lucretia transformed them into a myriad crickets. Hailing Fiola as their king, she placed him at their head, and reminding him solemnly that persistence conquers where force must fail, bade him lead them back to the forest.

In an incredibly short time this aerial army arrived at the castle of the Sorcerer with the Seven heads. It stood in the midst of a dense thicket, surrounded by a moat, the lurking place of demons with long forked tongues, and eyes that shot evil fires. Undaunted by their snarls, the crickets flew over the draw-bridge, and finding a way into the castle through the close-barred windows, swarmed round the Sorcerer's head. A cauldron swung from the domed ceiling, over a quenchless fire, and in this the wretch was even then concocting a potion by which he should overcome Fiorita. Her purity had hitherto protected her, and though he had bound her body with chains, he could not fetter her spirit.

'How dare you disturb me?' he roared, lunging at the crickets vainly with a long and glittering knife.

Fiola would fain have slain him where he stood, but when, forgetting his impotence, he hurled himself forward at the monster, he only tickled his nose.

'Leave him to us!' cried his cricket friends; and then they began their witch-song of '*Cree-cree-cree.*'

Now the Sorcerer having seven heads—Greed, Envy, Spite, Malice, Passion, Jealousy, and Despair, each of which would have instantly sprung forth again had Fiola been able to chop it off—he had naturally fourteen ears, and these were so extraordinarily sensitive to noise that he had destroyed all the woodpeckers in the forest that he might not hear their tap-tap on the trees as they searched the bark for insects.

He tickled the Monster's Nose.

You can judge, then, of his disgust when on his refusal to obey Lucretia's command, and break the bonds which held Fiorita, this host of crickets swarmed round his head, and filled the air with discord. Each pitched his voice in a different key, and the din of battle was as nothing to that which now pervaded the castle.

These were the words of the witch-song:

'Cree-cree-cree-cree
Set Fiola's Princess free.
Sorcerer thou, but Witches we—
Cricket-Witches, from grass and ditches.
Cree-cree-cree-cree!
Peace thine ears no more shall know
Till thou bidst the lady go.
Cree-cree-cree-cree!
Sorcerer, set the lady free!' [3]

Over and over again they chanted this lay, and every cricket, far and near, joined in the maddening chorus. They sang until the Sorcerer with the Seven Heads felt that his senses were leaving him; pallid with rage, he severed the White Princess's chains. By the power of Lucretia, who had clearly foreseen his discomforture, the moment that the chains fell from her Fiorita immediately became a cricket also, and gladly did she fly to the side of the Prince, who greeted her with rapture.

All would now have been well had they straightway left the castle, for Lucretia waited outside to restore to them their human form. As Fiorita passed the great cauldron which still swung over the lamp, she could not resist the temptation to lean over and peep inside, and the fumes from the potion being very strong, she straightway fainted, falling into the midst of the blood-red liquid. Before it could wholly cover her, the Cricket King seized her wings in his mouth; he carried her thus into the open air, where she speedily revived. Great was Lucretia's concern, however, when she heard from Fiola what had happened.

'Alas,' she sighed, 'not even I, who am mistress of spells and enchantments, can avert from Fiorita the consequences of her delay. Since the Sorcerer's potion touched her, for six months each year she must be a cricket, even as now; for the rest, she will be the White Princess, to dwell with you where you will.'

Then Fiorita was sad indeed, for she had lost her longing to see the land Beyond, and desired nothing better than to wed the Prince. But now that he knew she loved him, no spell could dampen Fiola's joy.

'While you are a cricket,' he said, 'I will be one too, for so long as you are beside me—what matters else?' And the Fays and Witches, who reverence all true love, elected to share their banishment.

And so it was, and is to this present time. For half the year Fiola is the Cricket King, and Fiorita, more than content, his Queen. But as Ascension day comes round, the spell is broken, and they take their accustomed places at the Court. It is hard to say when they are the happier; for love is as much at home in the humblest corner of Mother Earth as it is in a lordly Palace."

One night there was not a breath of air, and I could not sleep. I tossed this way and that for hours, and directly the birds began to twitter, I put on my things and slipped back the bolt of the grand hall door. Once outside, it was beautifully fresh and cool, and the clouds in the sky were like wreaths of pink flowers on a turquoise sea, arched over with gleaming gold. They changed every moment, and while I watched them I forgot to look where I was going. When I stopped at last I found myself in the middle of the market place, where I had been with Father the day before.

It was empty now, for no one was yet awake but me.

Among the quaint old wooden houses I noticed one that I had not seen before; at first it seemed to be indistinct, but the longer I stared at it, the clearer it grew. Over the door of the tiny shop was the figure of a hen cut into the stone, and while I was wondering who had carved it, the wings fluttered gently toward me. The bird moved its head, and its wings were lifted; it flew to the ground, and a lovely white hen was at my feet. It looked at me wistfully, and flew away; when I turned to the little house once again, it was not there. But beside me stood the Fairy Godmother.

"Come and sit in the shade," she said, when I asked her what had become of the hen, "and I will tell you all about her. She is seeking Furicchia, whom she served so well, not knowing that she is a shadow too."

The Enchanted Hen.

"Furicchia," said the Fairy Godmother, "was a very poor woman who owned a hen which an innkeeper greatly coveted. The shape of the bird was perfect; it had a most melodious voice, and its feathers were glossy and white as snow.

'Come now, good dame,' the man cried, persuasively, 'I will give you double the market value of your little hen, for I wish to make a present of her to the widow Ursula, whom I intend to espouse.'

'But the widow might kill and eat her!' said Furicchia, looking lovingly at the little hen, which she had brought up by hand from a tiny chick. It had slept beneath her best silk 'kerchief, and taken its food from her lips.

'That is as may be,' he replied. 'Come, Furicchia, I make you a handsome offer. Give me the hen, and you shall fare well next feast day.'

But Furicchia would not listen, in spite of the sad fact that her cupboard was as empty as her netted purse. The little hen was dear to her, though as yet it had lain no eggs, and she would not sacrifice her to her needs.

Ere evening came, Coccodé was clucking gaily under the kitchen table, and Furicchia found, not one egg, but three, all a rich coffee brown, and polished like porcelain. Having joyfully exchanged one with a neighbour for a dish of broth, she broke the second into it, and prudently saving the third for next day, thankfully made a good meal. When morning came, she found eggs to the number of a round dozen strewn about her tiny room, and from being almost on the verge of starvation, she had plenty now and to spare. For Coccodé, the grateful creature, laid eggs by the score, and not only were they of exquisite flavour and very large, but it was noticed that if sick folk ate them, they straightway returned to health.

Furicchia was now a famous egg-wife, and the more eggs she sold, the more eggs Coccodé laid. The little hen was both willing and industrious, and loved her kind mistress so dearly that she was never so happy as when helping to make her fortune. Her pride in Furicchia's first silk gown was comical to witness; she rustled her wings against its handsome folds, and clucked so loudly that the neighbours heard, and came to see what was the matter.

This silken gown it was that roused the anger of the Signora, a wealthy woman who had much, and knew no better than to want more. Hearing of the prodigious number of eggs which Furicchia supplied, though no one had ever seen her with other than a single hen, she set afoot much scandal concerning her, ending by declaring her to be an evil Witch. At this, Furicchia's neighbours began to look askance at her; but the eggs were so good, and so moderate in price, that on second thoughts they decided to treat the Signora's hints with the contempt which they deserved.

This made the lady still more angry; she resolved to find out Furicchia's secret, and ruin her if she could, so that she might obtain her customers for her own eggs. Coccodé was quite aware of what was going on, and before her mistress went out one morning she bade her fetch certain herbs that grew on a corner of barren land, and put these on the fire in a pot of wine.

'And now, dear mistress,' she continued, when all had been done as she said, 'do you go out and trust your luck to Coccodé.'

Furicchia had not long been gone, when the Signora's crafty face peeped slyly round the door. Finding the room apparently empty, she hurried in, delighted at such an opportunity for prying. First she peered here, and then she peered there, ransacking Furicchia's chests, and even turning over the leaves of her holy books, that she might see if an incantation to Witches had been written therein. Finally, she raised the latch of the inner chamber, where she had heard Coccodé clucking.

'I have found out Furicchia's secret now,' she thought with glee. 'Her little white hen is under a spell, and she and it shall be burnt as Witches.'

Coccodé was sitting on a pile of eggs that reached almost up to the ceiling, and even as she clucked she was laying more. The Signora drew close to her, and listened with all her ears, for she had distinguished words amidst her cluckings, and immediately jumped to the conclusion that Coccodé believed herself to be addressing her mistress. This is what she heard:

'Coccodé! now there are nine!
Bring me quickly the warm red wine.
Coccodé! take them away
Many more for thee will I lay.
And thou shalt be a lady grand,
As fine as any in the land,
And should it happen that any one

Drinks of the wine as I have done,
Eggs like me she shall surely lay;
This is the secret, this is the way,
Coccodé! Coccodé!'

[4]

'Aha!' said the Signora joyfully, 'now I have it!' And running back to the outer room, she lifted the wine off the fire and drank it, every drop, though it scalded her throat and made her choke. As it coursed through her veins she felt a most extraordinary sensation, and hurried home as quickly as she could. A meal was laid on the table, but she found great difficulty in taking her usual place, and could eat nothing but some brown bread, which she pecked at in a most curious manner. As the charm began to work, her legs grew thinner and thinner, and her feet so large that she had to cut off her boots. Next, her brown silk dress became a bundle of draggled feathers, while her nose turned into a beak, and her voice into a discordant cluck; in short, she was just a scraggy brown hen, and her friends held up their hands in horror. Eggs she laid by the score, but before she could sit on them they turned to mice and ran away. So she had nothing for all her trouble; and though she possessed a handsome house, she could only perch in a barn.

This is what comes of greed and envy, and of meddling with other people's business."

Just at this moment a girl darted out of a doorway opposite, followed by an elderly woman who loudly reproved her for refusing to do her share in some household task. Shrugging her shoulders, she came to a sudden end, as if she knew that her breath was wasted, and the girl disappeared with a peal of laughter.

"She is off to gossip instead of work," said the Fairy Godmother disapprovingly. "She will pay for it later, will pretty

Ursula, for the Fates are not likely to interfere on her behalf as they did for Pepita."

I had to coax her to tell me this story, for she said she had much to do, and could not stay. But when she heard that the very next day Father and I were leaving Italy, she refused no more. We sat down on the step of a splendid church, and no one seemed to notice us.

The Favourite of the Fates.

"Troubles rolled off Pepita as water from a duck's back. So lighthearted and full of good humour was she that nought ever seemed to vex her, and no one living had ever heard an unkind word fall from her rosy lips. Even the three grim Fates, who rule over mortal destinies, relaxed their stern brows as they looked down on her, and smiled indulgently.

Pepita was slender as a swallow, with a warm red flush on her olive cheeks, and dainty hands that looked far too delicate and small for even the lighter household tasks. These, indeed, Pepita seldom attempted, singing instead from morn to eve, and charming her mother with soft caresses when she hardened her heart and tried to scold her.

But Pepita could spin. Ah yes, she could spin, and as no other maiden had ever been known to do since Arachne was changed into a spider. The snowy flax flew from under her fingers as though her distaff were enchanted; which, indeed, was the case, for the wayward Fates had bestowed upon her a magic gift, and having given her this, not even they could take it away from her.

Pepita's mother was often wroth with her, for the dame had much work on her hands, and sighed that her only daughter should give her so little help. Were the maiden sent to wash clothes in the stream, ten chances to one they would go floating down the current while she twisted flowers in her hair. Were she set to make sweet little chestnut cakes, she would forget to put a cool green leaf at the bottom of each round baking dish, and when they were taken out of the ashes, behold, they would be all burnt!

'You are a good-for-nothing!' her mother would cry angrily; but this was not true, for Pepita could spin.

One feast day, while her mother went to the fair, she was told to watch the *pentola*, and to stir it carefully if it boiled too fast. It was made of rice and good fresh meat, with vegetables from the little garden; and it smelt so delicious that Pepita's small nostrils quivered like the petals of a rose on a windy day.

'I will taste it to see that all is well,' she murmured, and drawing back the iron pot, she helped herself to a liberal portion.

The *pentola* was good; Pepita tasted it yet again, for she had been up early to go to Mass, and had sung herself hungry on the way home. Soon there was no meat left.

'Ah, what shall I do?' she sighed, 'My mother will scold me terribly, and will tell the Padre that I am greedy.'

She was sighing still when her eyes fell on an old leather shoe which had been cast away behind the door. Her face all dimpled with mischief, Pepita soused this under a tap, and threw it into the soup.

'They will but think that the meat is tough!' she cried with a burst of laughter; but as the shoe fell into the boiling liquid her mother crossed the threshold.

'What have you done?' demanded she, peering into the pot. '*Madonnamia!* Was ever an honest woman cursed with such a daughter?' And breathing out angry hopes that an Ogre would come and take her, she drove Pepita out of the house.

At that moment a rich young merchant was strolling by, and Pepita unwittingly rushed into his arms. A thing such as this had never happened to him before, and since he scarce knew what to do, he clasped her tightly while he considered. By the time he released her, Pepita's face was pink as apple blossom, and the tears that sparkled on it were for all the world like dewdrops on the petals of a flower. Something stirred in his breast, and he blushed even more than she; for when a man falls suddenly in love he knows not where he stands. Looking from one to the other, the wrath of Pepita's mother suddenly cooled.

'Take her to wife,' she said, 'and you'll not get a bad bargain. True, she is nought in the house, but she can spin. And with all her faults she is not a scold.'

'One wants more in a wife than that!' said the merchant shrewdly, though the last of her statements went far with him, since his mother had a tongue. Looking into Pepita's eyes, which were heavenly blue, and sweet as an angel's, he lost his last qualm of doubt, and lifted her hand to his lips. Then he turned once more to the elder woman. 'I have vowed to my mother I will not wed without her free consent, but if your daughter meets with her approval, I will gladly do as you say.'

Pepita rushed into his Arms.

Guido's mother was in her seventieth year, and though she had never beheld a face more winning than merry Pepita's, it did not please her, and she gave her mind to finding a task which would prove beyond her powers.

'The garden paths are green with weeds,' she quavered; 'they have been sadly neglected since Pietro fell ill. Take the hoe, and root them up; leave not a single one.'

'Nay, mother! I seek not a gardener for my wife!' her son protested hotly, for Pepita's small hands could barely lift the hoe, and he had set his heart on her.

'Unless the paths be clear of weeds ere the sun sets, I will not give thee my consent,' said the old woman obstinately; and there was nothing left for Pepita to do but to hoe up the weeds as best she could.

No sooner had Guido's mother ceased watching her from the window, than Pepita whistled gently, and swift at her call came the birds she had fed with crumbs when the fields were bare. Pointing to the weeds, she made signs to them to destroy them, and by the time the old mother awoke from her nap, not one was left behind. This vexed her instead of giving her pleasure, for she did not wish her son to marry, and telling her maids they might have a holiday, she commanded Pepita to prepare the evening meal.

The maiden was now in much perplexity, for she knew not how to cook, and her experience that morning with the *pentola* had taught her little. But the Brownies who dwelt behind the hearth, and love to see a fair young face bending over the pots and pans, bade her be not discouraged, for they would stand her friends.

Then the nimble little men flew hither and thither, fetching garlic and oil and meat and rice in just the proportions that Guido loved, and adding certain secret flavours of their own until the smell of the broth made the old woman's mouth water, and she could not but praise Pepita's cooking. When it came to the time to test her skill at spinning, she was completely reconciled to her son's choice, and put no obstacles in the way of the wedding.

And now Pepita sang more blithely than ever, for though he was less well favoured, and slower of speech than many a young man who had wooed her, she adored her husband. She was as happy as the day was long until, wishing to have the biggest bank account as well as the prettiest wife in the neighbourhood, he took it into his head to turn her talent for spinning to account, and kept her beside her distaff from morn till eve.

‘I shall soon, at this rate, be richer even than the notary,’ he thought, as he looked delighted at his stores of flax; and Pepita besought him in vain to give her a little rest, for he could be as obstinate as his mother.

It was now that the Fates interfered on her behalf, though many more worthy than she are left to shift for themselves.

‘She has lost her bloom!’ sighed one grim sister.

‘Her cheeks are hollow!’ observed the second.

‘Her songs are sad ones!’ said the third with a dreadful frown. And then they put their heads together, and formed a plan whereby Guido might be outwitted.

As he sat in the doorway that evening while Pepita span, denying himself the sight of her in order that her work might not be disturbed, there came up the garden path a hideous old hag, who besought him to give her alms.

‘Look at me, Signor!’ she groaned, lifting her head so that he saw the wrinkled folds that lapped her chin. ‘Once I was fair as your Pepita, but I sat so long at my spinning wheel, that all my comeliness left me.’

Guido hastily gave her a coin, and urged her to begone; for he did not want Pepita to see her, or to hear what she had to say.

Next eve came a second old woman, uglier, if possible, than the last, and bent like some brutish beast. She had the same story to tell him of bygone loveliness, and Guido sped her down the hill with even more haste than before.

The next night a third old woman appeared, so dread of aspect that he was obliged to avert his gaze. Against his wish, he felt himself constrained to enquire the cause of her terrible affliction.

‘I sat at my wheel, good master,’ was the reply, ‘until beauty and sight both left me, and my skin became even as you see.’

Now thoroughly alarmed, he dismissed her quickly with a handful of coins, and calling Pepita to him, gazed at her long and searchingly. When the flush that his now unaccustomed touch had brought to her sweet face faded, he saw she was pale and thin. Her mouth drooped sadly, and purple shadows brooded round her eyes. With a cry of remorse he drew her to his breast, and kissed her tenderly.

'You shall spin no longer, my Pepita,' he said, 'for I would rather have you as you are than be rich as Satan himself!'"

And this was the very last story I heard. We started for home next morning, and I went to school at the half term—a ripping school where there was any amount of cricket, and so many other games that I had no time to think of Fairies.

But some day I'm going to find the Peri, and those other wonderful Sprites and Goblins of which Titania told me when I met her in the wood that Christmas day.

END OF THE BOOK

Footnotes:

[1] The Fairy Mythology

[2] Crane's Italian Fairy Tales

[3] Crane's Italian Fairy Tales

[4] Leyland's 'Legends of Florence'

Zeitfracht Medien GmbH
Ferdinand-Jühlke-Straße 7
99095 Erfurt, Deutschland
produktsicherheit@kolibri360.de